TRANSFORMING
ORGANIZATIONS

TRANSFORMING ORGANIZATIONS

Engaging the 4Cs for powerful organizational learning and change

MICHAEL ANDERSON and
MIRANDA JEFFERSON

BLOOMSBURY BUSINESS
LONDON • NEW YORK • OXFORD • NEW DELHI • SYDNEY

BLOOMSBURY BUSINESS
Bloomsbury Publishing Plc
50 Bedford Square, London, WC1B 3DP, UK
1385 Broadway, New York, NY 10018, USA

BLOOMSBURY, BLOOMSBURY BUSINESS and the Diana logo are trademarks of
Bloomsbury Publishing Plc

First published in Great Britain 2019

Cover design by Eleanor Rose
Cover image © Getty Images

Library of Congress Cataloging-in-Publication Data
Names: Anderson, Michael, 1969– author. | Jefferson, Miranda, author.
Title: Transforming organizations : engaging the 4Cs for powerful organizational learning
and change / Michael Anderson and Miranda Jefferson.
Description: London ; New York, NY : Bloomsbury Business, 2018. |
Includes bibliographical references.
Identifiers: LCCN 2018033028| ISBN 9781472949318 (hardback) |
ISBN 9781472949325 (export/airside) | ISBN 9781472949356 (exml)
Subjects: LCSH: Organizational change. | Organizational learning.
Classification: LCC HD58.8 .A684 2018 | DDC 658.4/06–dc23
LC record available at https://lccn.loc.gov/2018033028

ISBN: HB: 978-1-4729-4931-8
         ePDF: 978-1-4729-4934-9
         eBook: 978-1-4729-4933-2

Typeset by RefineCatch Limited, Bungay, Suffolk
Printed and bound in Great Britain

To find out more about our authors and books visit www.bloomsbury.com
and sign up for our newsletters.

Transforming Organizations *is dedicated to our families and for those who care about making organizations relevant and vital.*

CONTENTS

FIGURES

TABLES

FOREWORD

In his book *The Consolations of Economics* the British economist Gerard Lyons suggests that the success of any future economy will depend on what he calls the 3Cs – cash, commodities or creativity[1]. Without much in the way of cash or commodities the United Kingdom is increasingly dependent on the value of its Creative Industries, which generate over 6% of Gross Value Added[2] and will generate one million new jobs by 2025. The capabilities to continuously imagine, reinvent, innovate, design, disrupt conventional routines and processes and produce new products and experiences is at the core of these industries' success and now also characterise what is being called the creative economy. Which contributes 10% of the UK's GVA. The rise of the creative industries in the UK and elsewhere is no accident. In an uncertain and often volatile world, successful organisations and their leadership must embrace ambiguity, disruptive change, risk, and the exponential quickness of the digital 4th industrial revolution. A revolution that also depends on connectivity – of ideas, people, markets, expertise, production processes – both at the local level of creative clusters in many of our cities and towns and in the transglobal digital sphere. Connectivity requires highly skilled communicators, mutual respect and trust, culturally sensitive collaborations.

Additionally, both corporate, public, social enterprise and charitable organisations of all sizes are coming to understand the importance of ethical, humane and environmentally conscious decision making. McKinsey has shown that diversity at all levels of an organisation is both good for business and good for society – bringing cognitive, ethnic, cultural, gender and other differences together seeds change – new ideas, new challenges to the status quo[3]. Diversity is the social engine of creativity but diversity also brings extraordinary challenges in terms of conflicts of perspective, communication, collaboration and how we critically reflect on an organisation's mission and values.

Let's pause, as this book so often does, to think about how this all looks in practice. Let's remember the billions wiped of the share value of Facebook and VW in 2017/18 when they ruthlessly pursued profit over people and the environment. VW added to its woes by failing to recognise - to critically reflect on - the consequences of cheating diesel emissions tests without consideration of the environmental and health outcomes. Instead they were then caught testing foul emissions on caged monkeys and humans and claimed this was being done for social and environmental concerns. Facebook sought to monetise their users – turning them into data products to be sold, without ethical care, in the market place. In so doing Facebook lost money, users and risked confidence in the western democratic process.

A more positive case is JD.com, or Jingdong, sometimes called the Chinese Amazon, which is now the world's third largest tech company[4]. There are stark differences between life in China's tier one and two cities and remote agricultural areas. For many of the rural poor, moving to the cities is necessary for work and to overcome the lack of opportunity, resources and infra-structure. Very few have computers but everyone has a smart phone, many with a JD app. There are no Walmarts or hyper-markets. So, JD decided to expand through e-commerce, recruiting local drivers, strategically placed warehouse workers and more. It delivers by drones as well as more conventional means to quickly reach even the most distant communities and expects to double its existing market through this expansion into rural areas. It builds on its reputation for reliability and authentic rather than counterfeit products. A commercial, social and environmental success.

Liu Qiandong is the CEO of JD. Mark Zuckerberg is the CEO of Facebook. In his 1953 essay *The Hedgehog and the Fox,* Isaiah Berlin outlined two different human dispositions– the fox knows many things and the hedgehog one big thing[5]. The fox adapts to, shapes and learns from many experiences. It is emotionally literate, multi-talented and curious. It is quick agile and smart. The hedgehog relies on its one big thing and trusts that this one big thing is enough to survive and expand – it does not adapt to change, or seek other alternatives. Which CEO is the hedgehog and which the fox?

The beating and often restless heart of creative, collaborative, critically reflective organisations is the creative worker and teams. This book offers insights into different models of leadership practice and processes that encourage every member of an organisation:

- To develop their levels of social intelligence required to tolerate differences and negotiate, accept and reject the development and formation of ideas with sensitivity and respect found in the work of Teresa Amabile[6] and Daniel Goleman.[7]

- To develop ideas through processes of Research and Development, to test these ideas and evaluate their own performances against others without fear of failure found in the work of Stiglitz and Greenwald[8]

- To extend their own comfort zones in order to take on new experiences and ideas that destabilise the 'norms' of everyday work and the conventional methods of operating in social contexts found in the work of Mihai Csikszentmihalyi[9]

- To work productively without direct instructions and coercive management, to be self-motivated drivers of innovation, seeking a common objective rather than needing to control or be controlled reflected in Manville and Ober and Bilton's research[10]

- To practise models of leadership that encourage innovation, risk-taking and ideas rather than impose regulated and uniform protocols and procedures discussed by Carol Dweck[11] and Axon, Friedman, Jordan [12].

In response to Lyon's 3Cs the authors powerfully identify the 4C's of Creativity, Critical Reflection, Communication and Collaboration as being essential to our future economic, social and environmental needs. What I'm emphasising here is the vitality and vital importance of the 4Cs as they are articulated in this book. They are foundational and future proofing concepts for imagining and realising continuous transformational change in organisations that are more or less committed to a triple bottom line – looking to develop economic, social and environmentally conscious innovations, or as the authors have it creative processes. These concepts are closely intertwined and are as much based in surfacing and developing human capacities and capabilities as they are in economics. The fox knows many things and the 4Cs provide anchors for encouraging reflective, creative, collaborative and communicative gathering and focussing on ethical innovation and agile organising. Increasing complexity requires increasing clarity about organisational values, purposes and human as well as economic priorities. Without these anchors, organisations may fatally stick to their one big thing or be too slow and undecided about change.

The real value of the book is in the chapters that help us to see how to walk the talk – to turn concepts of the 4Cs into processes of change. This is done through stories and commentary – carefully selected and analysed case studies which allow us to sense how applying the foundational concepts have transformed different kinds of organisations with different needs and aspirations. These stories invite us to reflect on transformational organisational change. They provide practical starting points for any organisation to being or reflect on the opportunities for growth and change. The case studies are interspersed with clear frameworks of guidance; helping us to recognise change as a carefully considered process not an event; helping us to move from what we know to what we do. Unpacking for us the stages and characteristics of creative reflection; the skills required for effective collaboration and the elements of successful communication.

If the big C for the world is now creativity, the related concepts of critical reflection, collaboration and communication are its vital corollaries for economic as well as social and environmental action.

Professor Jonothan Neelands

University of Warwick Business School

ACKNOWLEDGEMENTS

Some of *Transforming Schools: Creativity, Critical Reflection, Communication and Collaboration* has been adapted for this book.

We would like to acknowledge the following friends and family who assisted in the development of this work with suggestions, feedback and advice: Carol Anderson, Dan Bell, Jamie Gerlach, Mike Dicker, Michael Jensen and Henry Anderson. We would also like to thank the team at Bloomsbury publishing for their patient and careful advice throughout the writing and publishing process.

Yes, Prime Minister © Jonathan Lynn and Antony Jay, 1986.

Yes Minister © Jonathan Lynn and Anthony Jay, 1982 by permission of Alan Brodie Representation Ltd (www.alanbrodie.com).

The following figures remain the property of 4C Transformative Learning and are reproduced here with permission:

3.3 The coherence makers for collaboration, communication, creativity and critical reflection

3.4 The Leading Organizations Framework in the 4C approach

4.2 The Organizational Effectiveness Wheel

4.4 The Deep Learning Diamond

5.4 The Creativity Cascade

6.2 The Critical Reflection Crucible

7.2 The Communication Crystal

8.2 Collaboration Circles

9.2 The Transformation Tangle

These designs are reproduced with the permission of 4C Transformative Learning.

For updates and information about working with us go to: www.4corganizations. org

INTRODUCTION

It is probably a widespread fault of authors to think that they live in particularly critical times of change. The opening pages of books on organizational transformation (and this book is no exception) talk of 'waves of change' that are about to crash on humanity. Heraclitus famously said, sometime around 500 BCE, that "there is nothing permanent except change". So, in a sense, there is nothing new about us claiming that we are in a state of change. We are calling here for a re-alignment between the pace of change that we see in the world around us, and the way our organizations need to respond to meet the challenge of this change. Ironically, the changes we are calling for in this book are not necessarily new. Business leaders, politicians, academics and communities have been calling for Creativity, Critical Reflection, Communication and Collaboration (the 4Cs) to be more prominent for several decades, and these capabilities are in demand from employers in all sorts of organizations.

Many before us have called for the 4Cs to be more centrally embedded in our organizations. There is, however, a gap between the aspirations reflected in these discussions and what actually happens at a leadership level and at every other level of the organization. This occurs because aspiration is easy, but action is difficult, so this book aims to close that gap. Our intention is to demonstrate that the change we need can only take place if we recalibrate, re-orientate and reconnect organizations with the 4Cs. We think this will become possible when organizations have clear and practical strategies that can be applied across all functions of the organization.

The coherence makers that we discuss throughout (outlined in Chapter 3) are our approach to closing this particular gap. The coherence makers are products of research and practical application in real organizations engaging with transformation. The approaches contained in this book emerge from research drawn from business, economics, education, management, philosophy and our own experience and work with organizations that are transforming. The strategies outlined here are designed to provide a simple yet rich way to reconceptualize transformation and close the gap between rhetoric and reality.

Rhetoric does not make reality. In our view, mindful and wise action does. This book is mostly about action. It is about the 'how' of transformation, not just the what or the why (although we do discuss that too). In the following are some caveats and notes that may assist you as you navigate this book.

Our extensive and diverse experience with organizations has forced us to think broadly about the strategies we are proposing here so that they will be as relevant for a Fortune 500 company as they will be for an early child-hood centre or a space agency. We have tried to apply what we know from our experience, research, consultancy and teaching in education, MBAs, interdisciplinary studies and other areas with our first-hand experience of the transformation process.

Even though this book has the rather grand title of *Transforming Organizations* it cannot cover everything that relates to organizational transformation. In this sense, the book is better understood as the beginning of a conversation rather than an encyclopaedic coverage of transformation. As we have discussed, the strategies and approaches we have mentioned here emerge from real organizations as will become apparent from the many case studies we offer. These case studies are a reflection on how we see the 4Cs applied by others. We have also presented case studies of our own work in transforming organizations through the 4Cs. Sometimes we have changed the details of the examples we use to preserve the anonymity of those in the case studies.

There are several ways to read this book. It is designed to be read in chapter sequence but can be revisited chapter by chapter as you focus on collaboration or organizational effectiveness for instance. It should be understood, however, that the 4Cs are a model of holistic transformation. In our view organizations cannot transform if this approach is ad hoc or piecemeal. All of the Cs are mutually dependent on one another. In other words, you cannot for instance transform through creativity without developing capacities in critical reflection, collaboration and communication.

Transforming Organizations is structured so that the initial chapters set up the rationale and frameworks for transformation (Chapters 1–4). In these chapters, we focus on the importance of wisdom, deeper learning and re-imagined practice in organizational transformation (which we explore through paradoxes). We also introduce some key features in the 'how' of transformation by using coherence makers. Coherence makers are frameworks that, when employed by organizations, make intangible concepts understandable. Chapters 5–8 outline our approach to creativity, critical reflection, collaboration and communication and provide in-depth details of the coherence makers that frame that learning. Chapter 9 discusses how these approaches can be combined and applied to create sustainable transformation. We also discuss in Chapter 9 the implications of transformation.

We have provided here a précis of the chapters so you can see at a glance the way the book is organized.

Chapter 1: Transforming organizations

Chapter 1 outlines the 4Cs approach to transformation. We discuss the rhetoric/reality gap and how the 4Cs can provide strategies and capacities to bridge that gap. We present a case study of Lego who survived and subsequently thrived by learning, re-imagining practices and developing wise leadership.

Chapter 2: Understanding the big picture

The big picture for organizations is the social, community, economic and environmental changes that are happening externally and internally. In our view, the big picture matters because organizations are not islands. Their success and often survival often depends on their ability to understand the big picture. Chapter 2 sets out the issues that our society currently faces: chaos, contradiction and complexity.[1] We make a case for creativity, collaboration, critical reflection and communication being crucial to remaking organizations in postnormal times. Nokia's decline provides our case study in Chapter 2 and illustrates how fear can lead to organizational decline. We present the case for organizational transformation.

Chapter 3: Preparing the ground: preconditions for transformation

We open this chapter with a case study of Woolf Farming and Processing. We argue that transformation is only possible when the ground is fertile and prepared for the challenges of transformation. We discuss leading transformation through the Leading Organizations Framework which is a coherence maker. Coherence makers provide structure for intangible concepts to close the gap between rhetoric and reality. We also introduce the concept of paradoxical wisdom to explain how seemingly contradictory concepts can provide a deeper understanding of a process.

Chapter 4: Making transformation happen

In Chapter 4 we discuss the organizational learning processes that are required to make transformation happen. We introduce a case study exploring the transformation processes of the charity, Save The Children International. We present the Organizational Effectiveness Wheel (OEW) as a coherence maker that provides a focus on the capacities required for 4C transformation to happen in organizations. In this chapter, we also introduce the Deep Learning Diamond coherence maker to deepen learning in organizations through:

- agency – empowerment and self-direction;
- inquiry – valuing questions over answers;
- feedback – iteration with experimentation;

- experiences – emotional, relational and thinking capacities;

- relevance – in-context application.

To illustrate these approaches, we introduce a case study on the Glasgow Effect which exemplifies these processes.

Chapter 5: Creativity

We begin this chapter with a case study of eyewear start-up, Dresden Optics. Through their case we explain our coherence maker for creativity, the Creativity Cascade. We argue that a full understanding of creativity in organizations can drive effectiveness. As with the other three Cs, creativity overlaps, interacts and is dependent upon critical reflection, communication and collaboration.

Chapter 6: Critical reflection

Fundamentally, critical reflection relies on a deep and broad analysis that makes transparent each individual's and each organization's presuppositions and assumptions about knowledge and power. The chapter begins by presenting the story of Volkswagen's failure to critically reflect, and the ongoing ramifications of this failure. This chapter also considers how organizations can employ critical reflection to generate productive action. As a way of demonstrating how this can work in practice we introduce the Critical Reflection Crucible coherence maker.

Chapter 7: Communication

We discuss the partnership of IDEO and Cineplanet (based in Peru) as a case for how clear and true communication can make transformation possible. We introduce the Communication Crystal as a coherence maker that frames an approach to understanding and developing communication skills. A 'crystal' prism with its many surfaces and angles is used to describe communication, because, like a crystal, communication is multi-faceted, and refracts and reflects messaging in myriad ways.

Chapter 8: Collaboration

A premise of the 4Cs approach is that through collaboration humans become their fuller self. Through the mutuality of true collaboration, we expand who we are. To achieve such beneficial mutuality, however, requires the navigation of complex dynamics in communication and relationships. This chapter is about these dynamics. We present the case of the Johns Hopkins Community Health partnership to demonstrate what deep collaboration can achieve. We have synthesized collaborative processes into a coherence maker: Collaboration Circles. It is a supporting structure or scaffold to frame how collaboration can be learnt and facilitated.

Chapter 9: How 4Cs can close the rhetoric reality gap: some implications

We close the book by discussing how all of the features of 4C transformation work together. The Transformation Tangle coherence maker outlines the stages and phases of transformation and we discuss the realities and implications of making transformation a reality in organizations. This chapter argues that 4C transformation is achievable if the realities and challenges are understood and then effective 4C strategies are employed to respond.

When we began engaging with transformation we knew it was an ambitious task. The current climate of risk aversion and organizational intransigence has left us with many organizations that are becoming irrelevant or unresponsive to our current needs as a society. We never claim any of these changes are easy (quite the opposite). We have, however, in our discussions with organizations, sensed a desire for a new way ahead – a way that connects with the capacities that contribute to human thriving. We are experiencing critical changes in our society and our communities. We hope this book makes a contribution to developing relevant organizations that make a beneficial difference and a constructive contribution to developing authentic, wise and sustainable transformation.

1

Transforming organizations

Introduction: jumping the rhetoric reality gap

On 5 October 1979,[1] stuntman Kenny Powers (Figure 1.1) attempted to jump his rocket powered Lincoln Continental from Canada to the USA 1 mile (1.61 kilometres) across the St. Lawrence River. The preparation took more than four years, it was costly (more than one million dollars), methodical and exacting. When the day finally came for the jump the car flew 50 feet (15.24 metres) and plunged into the river seriously injuring the stuntman. In the end, no matter how

FIGURE 1.1 *Stuntman Kenny Powers before the 'big jump'.*

careful the preparation of the equipment or how experienced the team or highly trained the stuntman, they fell woefully short of the required goal. Fast forward to today and our organizations face a similar jump. We have spent years preparing ourselves, learning, restructuring, harmonizing, recruiting and developing the 'right' people. In our view, we currently do not have the capacity to make the jump. We need to bridge the gap between old ways of thinking and doing in organizations, to approaches that are going to help us move from rhetoric (creativity, innovation, effective and authentic collaboration, perceptive critical reflection and incisive communication) to the realities (complex problems, fixed mindsets and outmoded practices) facing us in an uncertain world. In this book we want to offer some preparations and processes for organizations to attempt this jump.

The rhetoric reality gap

There is a growing chorus from governments, shareholders, governors, business councils and academics about the need for our organizations to change. They variously argue (as we do later in the book) that changes in technology, work practices, the environment and society are creating an irresistible momentum for transformation. We will discuss transformation later in this chapter but in short, we are referring to the process of shifting practices and approaches to make them relevant to current realities. The problem is the 'rhetoric' hardly ever engages with the reality of organizations and transformation. In the end, this can lead to some organizations groping in the dark for how to transform or falling back on old practices. These approaches are often unsuited to new challenges and can lead to the decline and demise of some organizations. This book aims to begin closing that gap between the rhetoric of transformation and the action of transformation.

We will provide approaches and frameworks that make explicit the capacities required for organizations not only to survive but to thrive in circumstances that present new and dynamic challenges. Now more than ever we need organizations that can look over the incoming waves of compliance and administration to see a way forward, in a sometimes confusing, complex and chaotic world and construct a vision for change.

The 4Cs (creativity, critical reflection, collaboration and communication) form the basis of these approaches and are critical in moving our organizations away from being museums of outmoded practice. These 4Cs have the potential to make organizations energetic, flexible and resilient places that directly meet the needs of a world in flux. Like Kenny Powers (our stuntman) we are staring at a chasm between rhetoric (the what) and reality (the how). This book aims to bridge that chasm by offering tangible strategies, approaches and frameworks.

We believe it is time for a fundamental reconsideration of the way we do organizations. In all of our organizations, irrespective of their size, shape or motivation, we need to embed the capabilities that make them inherently wise, flexible, productive, innovative and resilient so we can ready them for an uncertain future and contribute to a world that is focused on human thriving and not disintegration. While we do not claim we have all the answers to this major challenge, we argue a renewed focus on the 4Cs is a critical part of making organizations equipped for the present and the future.

This chapter outlines our approach to transformation through learning and re-imagined practices. In most chapters of this book we begin with a case study of an organization that has engaged with transformation and has not only survived but thrived in the process. In this chapter, we tell the story of Lego's transformation to demonstrate how the 4Cs can work deeply in an organization to bring about transformation. Lego's transformation was enabled by learning and reflections on their practices. The application of effective and focused creativity, critical reflection, communication and collaboration was the difference between success and financial decline.

Transforming an organization through learning and wisdom

Perhaps like you, one of my[2] fondest memories of childhood was playing in a seemingly bottomless bucket of Lego (Figure 1.2). I remember the almost endless combinations I tried to build depending on what had caught my imagination that week, from superheroes to racing cars and castles. Lego as a product was and still is a standard part of a kid's first experience of play and innovation. Yet Lego (the company and the product) had a near death experience at the turn of the last century. Like so many other companies, new

FIGURE 1.2 *A bucket of Lego.*

competitors and innovations in the toy market were threatening to displace a brand that for so many years had been a standard part of childhood play. The legendary Lego, which had a steady and successful history, was now facing sales losses of 26 per cent in 2003 and 20 per cent in 2004.[3] Lego was looking at almost certain annihilation. The situation was summed up dramatically by the CEO Jørgen Vig Knudstorp at the time: 'We are on a burning platform, losing money with negative cash flow, and a real risk of debt default which could lead to a break-up of the company.'[4]

In part these problems were being created by an overly complicated product line with over 12,500 different components in stock, hundreds of different colours and 11,000 suppliers. In 2004 Lego acted. It created a diverse team of internal and external specialists[5] to collaborate and re-imagine the organization and head off catastrophe. The collaborators considered all aspects of the organization from supply chain to deliveries and customer satisfaction. In 2005 the team created a 'war room' to enact the 'shared vision' strategy with drastic effect. The company reduced the colours by half, and the stock units from 12,500 to 6,500. The company also communicated directly with its customers to critically reflect on its assumptions about the business. Discussions with the top twenty clients revealed 24-hour delivery was not essential. This change alone brought significant cost savings to the business. In 2015, although some of the product options were reduced, customers saw on-time delivery improve markedly. Because of these changes between 2005 and 2008, sales increased by 35 per cent and fixed costs reduced from 75 per cent to 33 per cent. In 2016, the company reported record revenue largely due to their investment in digital products and innovation. Lego's CEO said of this transformation in 2016:

Innovation is critical to our success and each year around 60 per cent of our portfolio is new products. We are constantly challenging ourselves to engage and inspire children with the most relevant, exciting and fun play experiences. This year we have strengthened our efforts around digital engagement and found new ways to connect with children online and through a range of digital platforms.[6]

In addition, Lego is now participating in partnerships with UNICEF to protect the rights of the child, and developing programmes for cyber safety and refugee education initiatives. In 2016 Lego's employees organized play experiences for more than 100,000 children[7] around the world in partnership with local children's charities.

Lego as a learning organization

The story of Lego's transformation is probably familiar to many. The key feature of this story for us is that this company learnt. It learnt through focused processes that built capacities in what are called the 4Cs: collaboration, creativity, critical reflection and communication. By learning we are referring to the ability of an entity to change and reshape in response to understanding the issues facing that organization. We will go into detail about how these processes can be enacted in organizations throughout this book. Briefly this is how these capacities were built and implemented in Lego's transformation.

Critical reflection

Critical reflection is the ability to perceive and analyse situations and then formulate wise responses to complex problems. Inherent to critical reflection is an individual's analysis of their agency. Agency is each individual's ability to develop insight and exercise control within a context, situation or organization. In Lego's case, critical reflection helped them to understand how their complex management structures and the sometimes confusing decision-making processes led to the slow decline of the organization. They were then able to act creatively to devise a strategy for transformation. Of course, reflection is not a new term to many of us, but reflection that analyses and prompts action in our experience of organizations is atypical. We discuss the uses of critical reflection in more depth in Chapter 6.

Creativity

Creativity is the innovation literacy as we argue in Chapter 5. Often when trouble arises, organizations tend to cut innovation and creativity rather than investing more heavily in them. In Lego's case the opposite occurred. They innovated their way out of trouble, relying on the capacities (creativity and innovation) to identify new products and markets that led to improvements in revenue. Companies that faced similar challenges to Lego, such as Kodak, did not act creatively enough in the face of rapid change.[8] These businesses have become cautionary tales demonstrating what happens when organizations cannot reorganize and have confidence in their creativity in the face of rapidly shifting business and societal realities. Organizations who cannot build creative capacity are unlikely to connect deeply with innovation. Lego's history of creativity, innovation and play may have been one of the deep cultural factors that allowed it to survive and is enabling it to thrive almost two decades later. Another capacity that made its transformation successful was communication.

Communication

The first instinct in Lego's case was not to talk but to listen. Interviewing its clients and being alert to their messages about deliveries provided them with the evidence they needed to streamline their processes. Once the organization listened it shared the vision and involved their community in the discussion. This might seem simple in hindsight but there are numerous organizational examples where communication is misunderstood as a one-way process. In Chapter 7 we expand and explain how organizations can build effectiveness by understanding and enacting effective communication strategies.

Collaboration

Instead of appointing a hero leader who swept in and slashed the organization, Lego trusted in collaborative processes. They developed a team who had wide-ranging expertise within the organization and worked together to make the changes. The establishment of the 'war room' and the 'shared vision' strategy situated the issue in Lego as a shared problem with a shared solution. In the implementation of the solution, divisions within Lego collaborated across functional areas to make systems and approaches more efficient. They also worked with their suppliers, retailers and customers to understand them more comprehensively. This kind of transformation occurs when true collaboration occurs (which is different in critical ways from co-operation and teamwork). We will discuss this further in Chapter 8.

Lego's experience demonstrates how central the 4Cs are to making transformation a reality and in their case avoiding potentially terminal decline. Lego's transformation experience demonstrates the 4Cs are not just vague aspirational concepts, they can be understood deeply and can be embedded in the culture of an organization. But this work takes will, energy, courage, determination, and most of all it takes an explicit understanding of how to develop and implement these sometimes elusive 4C concepts. We think the lessons from Lego chart the way forward. As an organization, it changed its shape after transformative learning, and it continues to learn and transform. In this way learning was made possible by using the 4Cs to critically reflect on the organization and then creatively to communicate and collaborate to bring about transformation.

Organizations in the twenty-first century will not face a steady state as circumstances will continue to change and pose dynamic challenges. The rapid evolution of technology and big complex societal changes mean our assumptions will need to be recast continually. Lego's survival and subsequent success demonstrates the need for organizations to invest in understanding and applying the 4Cs in their processes, relationships and partnerships. But before we go much further let us identify some of our own assumptions, such as what we mean by the terms 'transforming' and 'organizations'.

An organization

We have both worked and continue to work in different kinds of organizations. We work with universities, businesses, governments, schools, non-governmental organizations and religious organizations to name but a few. The one thing we notice is their need to come to grips with becoming entities that learn. This book is not called 'Transforming Businesses' or 'Transforming NGOs'. This book is called *Transforming Organizations* because what all of these entities have in common is far more substantive than that which divides them. As many sociologists argue there is more in common than is distinct between different organizations nowadays. Organizational researchers, Bromley and Meyer argue:

> As traditionally separate sectors shift toward formal, and more standardized, forms of organization, the historical distinctions between them come to increasingly rest in legal and scientific definitions rather than in functional purposes. Today, we know a non-profit is such because it has the appropriate legal status. It becomes harder and harder to determine an organization's form (business, government, or charity) based on functional activity alone.[9]

For us and for the purposes of working out whether or not you work and live in an organization (and if this book applies to you) we offer this definition. Organizations are bound by a social contract that brings individuals together to organize and create structures, relationships, cultures, climates, ideas and services. These activities enrich human capacity and agency to contribute to the growth of a wise, civil, fair and just, democratic and vibrant society.

You may notice that we have made a moral judgement here. There are plenty of entities that may be considered organizations but are focused on human or social disintegration, rather than flourishing. The Mafia for instance is not concerned necessarily with the emergence of the common good, nor with justice, fairness and wisdom. A necessary requirement for the organizations we work with is that they are interested in building rather than eroding communities and individuals. Having defined organizations what do we mean by organizational transformation?

Organizational transformation

Transformation has become a buzzword in organizations in the same way as terms such as disruption, deep dive, core competency, strategize, socialize, incentivize, outside the box and bleeding edge. Words used in this kind of way become somewhat meaningless due to overuse (they are often called exhausted signifiers). This is particularly so for a word like transformation. For us, transformation is the often slow process of moving from current ways of working to adapting to new and emerging circumstances. We are not advocating throwing the 'baby out with the bathwater'. The resources and capacities for transformation often lie within the organization. The skills, knowledge and understanding organizations have gained over years of learning and experience should not be discarded but rather they should be reshaped to meet the challenges organizations face. These transformations do not happen quickly and they are often difficult. Where they do happen, the whole organization commits resources and energy to the task of transformation. These organizations make hard decisions because they understand that transformation means survival. They would prefer to be in the position Lego is in today rather than Kodak.

The 'how' of transformation

Most of the rest of this book is focused on the 'how' rather than the 'why' of transformation. The 'why' will be covered for the most part in Chapter 2. In our experience, transformation is delivered through transformative leadership, deep organizational learning, wisdom and re-imagined practices. Here is a brief description of each of these themes.

Transformative leadership

Transformative leadership is a characteristic or quality and it is intrinsically collaborative – not just present in one person. The 4Cs are implicit in transformative leadership, so the organization with transformative leadership will be explicitly creative, collaborative and critically reflective with open multi-way communication. More critically, these features will be evident throughout the organization and not just at the 'top', 'middle' or 'bottom'. The transformative leader develops a culture that deeply embeds the 4Cs and this enables the organization to respond effectively to environmental, economic or social changes wisely and swiftly. The leadership in these organizations have mindsets, structures and processes that:

- can imagine the future (creativity);
- relate to and value others in a multi-way exchange (communication);
- reflect on assumptions and established practices (critical reflection);
- employ and enable the genius of the collective (collaboration).

These inherently agile qualities lead to an organization that does not stand still as the world whizzes by. These organizations can re-imagine the possible but can also learn deeply from their own experience.

Deep organizational learning

Peter Senge's book, *The Fifth Discipline: The Art and Practice of the Learning Organization*[10] argues that the benefits of learning are linked to an organization's capacity for strategic success and strategic renewal.[11] He claims, 'the organizations that will truly excel into the future will be the organizations that discover how to tap people's commitment and capacity to learn at all levels of the organization'.[12] In a dynamic and competitive context, BP's CEO John Browne supports Senge's claims, 'Learning is at the heart of a company's ability to adapt to a rapidly changing environment. It is the key to being able both to identify opportunities that others might not see and to exploit opportunities rapidly and fully'.[13] The ability to exploit and explore learning is seen by many CEOs and learning specialists as beneficial to an organization's performance. But it is not just any kind of learning, the quality of the learning we are identifying is deep and wise.

Cal Newport's *Deep Work*[14] helps to define what deep learning actually looks like. His book focuses on the individual in the organization, but we think it applies to the organization as well (which after all is the sum of the individuals within it). He says: 'To remain valuable in our economy, therefore, you must master the art of quickly learning complicated things. This task requires deep work. If you don't cultivate this ability, you're likely to fall behind as technology advances'.[15] In Newport's analysis, superficial learning is not sufficient. Learning requires agility but it also requires the ability to look deeply into problems, challenges and opportunities. He argues, like psychologist Mihaly Csikszentmihalyi, that human beings are at their best when immersed deeply in something challenging.[16]

One of the features of our changing social and economic climate is the emergence of super complex questions and problems. In Newport's view and our own, the ability to deeply apply one's thinking to complicated ideas provides a pathway to effectiveness. For example, Lego's methodical collaborative and evidence-based approach to understanding their delivery processes was deep work that led to deep learning. Rather than just change their approach without evidence they listened to their retailers' views about the delivery times and understood the problem in depth. It is not, however, enough to learn deeply. Many organizations have used deep learning to construct better ways to oppress and destroy communities. Wisdom is essential to make organizations a constructive force in our community and our world.

Wisdom

Wisdom is essential to a civil society and the lack of it can be disastrous. The need for wisdom in organizations is highlighted by the spectacular examples of failure in institutions such as the demise of Barings Bank, Lehman Brothers, Fannie Mae and Freddie Mac. Wisdom is the moral, ethical and responsible action of a good citizen. Wisdom in an organization means being wise in the detail and wise in the bigger picture. We refer to altruism and acting for the greater good as requisite capacities in the Organizational Effectiveness Wheel in Chapter 3. These capacities are inherent to wisdom. To learn wisdom requires an approach that goes beyond being compliant to rules and regulations. The ancient philosopher Aristotle argued that wisdom is the way we exercise judgement and that it is deeply embedded in our character, learning and competence.[17] How then can we learn wisdom in an organization? We argue it begins by understanding deep learning. Deep learning is the process of going beyond the superficial, and understanding the deep-seated problems organizations face. Deep learning is made possible by building capacities in creativity, critical reflection, collaboration and communication, so organizations can move beyond knee-jerk and self-serving reactions and begin to develop deep analysis of problems and effective solutions. Organizations with these qualities are able to re-imagine their practices to meet the emerging needs of their clients, stakeholders, students or collaborating partners.

Re-imagined practices

Like the goldfish in the bowl, organizations rarely look deeply into the 'really why' of their practices. In a sense because these practices are the 'water organizations swim in' they are rarely questioned or re-examined. For example, workplace researchers Alveson and Spicer suggest market-research companies have 'stupid' practices that have become endemic and unquestioned:

> These knowledge-intensive firms typically hire well-mannered young people with decent degrees to do two things: call people while they are eating dinner to ask inane questions, or crunch the data that these phone calls yield. It is questionable just how much intellectual skill is required by either of these jobs. What they do require is a nice accent and thick skin. Small wonder that one call-centre operative described the job as 'an assembly line in the head.[18]

This persistence with potentially inefficient practice is widespread in our experience. These practices remain because often there are no incentives in a large organization to shift when practices have become endemic and unquestioned. Often a crisis like the profit downturn at Lego leads to transformative leadership. In Lego's case, much of the 'taken for granted' approaches of the company were questioned and then transformed to meet the emerging realities. When Lego reduced the colours by half and the stock units from 12,500 to 6,500 it challenged entrenched practice. This change alone vastly improved Lego's profitability and was one of the key factors in its survival. For Lego, re-imagining practice depended on thoughtful and perceptive leadership that engaged directly with asking tough questions about their assumptions and their entrenched practices.

As we mentioned at the beginning of this chapter, the chasm between rhetoric and reality needs to be bridged to transform our organizations. Unlike the story of stuntman Kenny Powers that began this chapter, we need to get ourselves and our organizations across the chasm. We think the 4Cs are critical to this preparation and Lego's experience supports this claim. Unlike many of the transformation approaches of the past, the strategies and frameworks we are presenting in this book focus on individual and organizational flourishing.

In our work with organizations, we invest deeply in relationships by engaging with them over long periods of time. We rarely run one day workshops, but rather we get alongside people and organizations to ensure the strategies, practices and approaches we suggest are context driven and deeply embedded through deep learning, wisdom and transformational leadership that leads to re-imagined practices. For us, these re-imagined practices are crucial if we are to see real and sustainable transformation in organizations. This deliberate and strategic approach can create a bridge from rhetoric to reality and deliver for organizations authentic and sustainable transformation.

The old approaches to transformation such as restructures or name changes without re-imagining practice seldom make organizations more relevant and dynamic. These changes are unlikely to be effective and durable in a world that is shifting before our eyes. If we care about the role of organizations in human flourishing we must ensure transformation works for everyone in the organizations and our communities.

The organizations we work with that flourish are able to learn, wisely lead and transform practices in response to the changing big picture – changing social, business, political and environmental circumstances. The challenge for organizations and individuals is not to be fearful of the present and future, but to seize the opportunities they present. We believe this becomes possible by embedding the 4Cs. In the next chapter, we describe the 'big picture' as we see it and outline the case for transformation.

2

Understanding the big picture

The wider context of change in our societies, communities and organizations – the big picture – is critical to the 'why' or the rationale for transformation. While the big picture may not seem relevant to some individuals and organizations, these shifting circumstances ultimately contribute to the challenges facing our organizations. Sometimes the broader context, such as rapid innovation by

FIGURE 2.1 *A Nokia product from their heyday.*

competitors, creates pressures that shape organizations for the better, or the worse, as we will see in the Nokia case study we feature in this chapter.

The strong winds of change in society, politics, economics, media, technology and other sectors are disrupting the way we live, and are relevant to every organization (and each individual employee, manager and leader in each of those organizations). Organizations can choose to transform in the face of the 'big picture' or become ineffective, sidelined, irrelevant and ultimately defunct (such as Nokia, Toys R Us, Kodak, Blockbuster Video etc.). In 2015 the Boston Consulting Group (BCG) reported that corporations survive only half as long as they did thirty years ago with most businesses in most industries dying younger.[1] They explain the new normal:

> business environments are increasingly volatile. They are also increasingly varied: from stable to unpredictable, from fixed to shape-able, from favourable to harsh. And conditions change with increasing speed: businesses move though their life cycles twice as quickly as they did 30 years ago.[2]

In other words, shifting circumstances require organizations to transform. The costs of transformation can be high but the costs of not transforming are apparent in Nokia's case.

Nokia: fear rather than transformation

Nokia is a multinational telecommunications company founded in 1865 that grew exponentially during the 1990s driven by innovative communications products (mobile phones etc.). At the time Nokia was the fastest growing technology company in the world.[3] That market dominance has now been overtaken by other players such as Apple but in the 1990s Nokia's dominance of the mobile phone market was seemingly unassailable. In the period from 2007 to 2012, however, the company went from riches to rags. Record high profit results were posted in 2007 but by 2012 Nokia was facing bankruptcy and was eventually acquired by Microsoft in 2014.[4] While there are various reasons for the decline of this once great company, most of the explanations come down to poor communication, hierarchical and bullying management and trading on perhaps the most basic of all human emotions: fear.

Fear started at the top with managers realizing that to compete with Apple they needed a more effective operating system, but could not admit that publicly 'for fear of appearing defeatist to external investors, suppliers, and customers and thus losing them quickly'.[5] The fear in this instance emerged because the 'big picture' of shifting market realities caused anxiety rather than opportunity. This fear turned Nokia in on itself.

The rapid evolution and market dominance of telecommunications companies like Apple and Samsung stunned Nokia, and in the face of fierce competition and innovation Nokia seemed unable or unwilling to transform its culture. Nokia's history demonstrates evidence of creativity and collaboration in the development of many 'cutting-edge' products that led to its market dominance. However, Nokia's tendency towards 'command and control' management created huge problems. In a recent study of Nokia's organizational culture, Professor of Strategy, Quy Huy made this observation:

> We were struck by the descriptions of some members of Nokia's board and top management as "extremely temperamental" who regularly shouted at people "at the top of their lungs". One consultant told us it was thus very difficult to tell them things they didn't want to hear. Threats of firings or demotions were commonplace.[6]

The fear-culture in Nokia was created by individuals who neglected to communicate and critically reflect. In the face of rapid change and fierce competition a company that had survived for well over a century was brought to its knees by human factors. This is often the case. Rarely is the demise or the slow disintegration of organizations caused by poor software, the wrong building or insufficient resourcing, although these can be contributing factors. In our experience, organizations thrive or decline because of humans and their capacity to respond with agility and wisdom to change. Nokia is one case that makes our point about the ever-presence of change. Extraneous factors such as software and buildings are enablers but in the end if organizations are not wise and do not learn, they will face a similar fate to Nokia.

In Nokia's case, not understanding the big picture created an environment of fear leading to rapid and dramatic disintegration. As Quy Huy puts it 'Nokia people weakened Nokia people and thus made the company increasingly vulnerable to competitive forces. When fear permeated all levels, the lower rungs of the organization turned inward to protect resources, themselves and their units.'[7] Nokia's lack of understanding of the big picture and how to respond to the changing conditions within that big picture led to organizational paralysis and a reliance on old practices. Instead of putting their faith in communication and critical reflection to drive creativity and collaboration they resorted to fear and threats.

The 4C approach to transformation (demonstrated in the Lego case, Chapter 1) critically analyses the issues and then works deeply to change the culture, practices and approaches by integrating and operationalizing creativity, critical reflection, collaboration and communication into the DNA of the organization. The 4C response to external challenges is to concentrate on explicitly building those skills. We argue throughout this book that creativity, critical reflection, communication and collaboration are crucial to reframing, re-imagining and remaking our organizations and helping our community to pro-actively respond to the big picture in postnormal times. We are arguing for a revolutionary transition for organizations that move them from places that rely on business as usual, to places that begin to concentrate on creating value for their communities by making their workplaces feature co-creativity, ingenuity and imagination. So, what is this imagined future ('the big picture') that makes these transformations so urgent?

Imagining the unimaginable

For some reason, it is very difficult for humans to imagine a future in ways other than it is at the moment. For instance, our not too distant ancestors thought human mechanized flight unlikely despite a series of rapid developments involving kites, balloons and gliders. In our everyday lives, we find it difficult to imagine it raining if we are in the middle of brilliant sunshine, even if weather forecasts predict a sudden storm. In some ways that lack of ability to foresee or imagine is at the heart of the challenge of future relevance for our organizations. Like the weather analogy, the forecasts are in. They predict a future that has both foul and fair weather and we need skills and capacities in our organizations to survive. We have entered into what sociologist Zygmunt Bauman calls a phase of liquidity 'in which all social forms melt faster than new ones can be cast. They are not given enough time to solidify, and cannot serve as the frame of reference for human actions and long-term life-strategies.'[8] These new social structures in some ways constrain us from imagining what the future might look like and may make re-imagining the future far more difficult than it ever has been before. Educator and philosopher Maxine Greene[9] argues that being able to imagine is a state of mind absolutely necessary to create what may be possible. In our work enabling organizational transformation, we notice that comfort-zones, fear, apathy and indifference can only be stirred and challenged by a belief in the power of imagination. Greene[10] describes the imagination as a space of freedom where humans are initiators and agents of an alternative reality. The imagination allows us to break from what we take for granted and to set aside the familiar.

The history of transportation provides a tangible example of how imagination can drive innovation and economic growth. When the Wright brothers first flew a powered plane on 17 December 1903 it was a triumph of engineering, but perhaps more critically it was an extraordinary act of the imagination. Their imagined innovation, created in the face of scepticism, made possible a multibillion-dollar industry that lies at the foundations of our society's now taken for granted mobility and productivity. For the Wright brothers the engineering skills were critical, but more crucial was the imagination of what innovation might be and could bring. While the Wright brothers had little in the way of business skill, they did, like many modern-day entrepreneurs, have the ability to imagine and innovate. They looked to and engaged with change rather than looking to 'business as usual' approaches. As business professors Komporozos-Athanasiou and Marianna Fotaki[11] argue, our society's wellbeing depends on organizations' ability to change and to imagine an alternative series of futures:

> The way in which we imagine the organizations we inhabit (through producing images, meanings and emotions) has a concrete effect on the actions we take within them when pursuing our individual goals and organizational objectives. Imagination is thus crucial for producing new realities . . . Without imagination, organizations cannot pursue new pathways challenging current dominant modes of representation.[12]

But while imagining transformation is hard, actually creating it in organizations in a time of rapid change is harder.

Renewing organizations: the case for transformation

Transformation is difficult and mostly painful. Many of us have become 'invested' in organizations through our time, money or attention. It often feels like we have been investing over and over in institutions and consequently we are terrified to stop doing what we have always been doing. Adding to the fear is the fact that we have been investing in old paradigms because we could not imagine what comes next – this is known in economics as 'the sunk cost' hypothesis. You can see elements of this kind of thinking in organizations that are careering headlong towards oblivion (Nokia) and yet nobody is able to point out the obvious, that an inability to change, often because of sunken costs and 'business as usual', means almost certain organizational decline. This would have been the fate of Lego had it not been for the wise leadership we discussed earlier. The demise of companies like Bear Sterns in the subprime mortgage crisis of 2007 and the subsequent global financial crisis or the long slow death of once famous newspaper mastheads (most famously the *News of the World*) by doing 'business as usual' in the face of a rapidly changing world are cautionary tales for those of us who care about transforming our organizations to make them future-ready. Of course, not all of this investment is lost as organizations continue to grow, change and evolve. Yet the demands of the twenty-first century make the changes seem more urgent, more imminent.

The ability to imagine and then re-imagine ourselves and our organizations has become more critical as we face massive social, economic and political change. The advent of globalization and the technological revolution have presented opportunities, as well as the disruption and fragmentation of communities. To some extent these changes have destabilised the 'old certainties' in our institutions (including our organizations) that we used to rely upon. We have the resources in organizations, we just require the will to transform in response to shifting conditions in our communities and our societies. So, what are the prevailing conditions (the big picture) in our society that demand change in our organizations?

The challenge of postnormality

While there is nothing new about corporate greed, contemporary capitalism and hyperactive market economies, all of these features have created globalized and networked economic misery causing diminishing levels of trust in organizations and institutions. These crises of confidence and crises of trust have developed in the midst of other crises: the crisis of international conflict, the crisis of climate change, the crisis of state sponsored terrorism, the crisis of food security and the crisis of mass refugee movements causing misery on an international scale. The rapid exchange of information that technology facilitates has created a 'perfect storm' of crises that are complex, contradictory and confusing. As economists Marshall and Picou suggest: 'The critical question is not how do we reduce uncertainty, but rather how do we make better decisions in a world of irreducible uncertainties?'[13] In this liquid, shifting context how do we understand the current reality? We need to look beyond the 'normalities' of the past and re-imagine our practices to ensure they are fit for purpose in a postnormal world.

Beyond 'normality'

The normality paradigm is an inadequate and to a large extent discredited starting point for organizations. Understanding the present and imagining the future of our organizations, we must not only take account of but work to 'build in' the features of postnormality (chaos, complexity and contradiction) into our assumptions. As we recognize the features of the big picture we can 'future-proof' our organizations for an uncertain future. The problem is organizations are almost universally focused on assumptions that arise from normality: hierarchy, standardization, cause and effect, economic growth, industrial prosperity and the profit motive. If we look to our education systems we see similar assumptions. There are vast testing and reporting regimes imposed by governments in Western economies such as Australia and the United Kingdom and many of the skills that are tested are still based on skills that are no longer relevant in postnormal times. The drive to do better with old thinking is akin in our view to perfecting steam train technology – nice to do, but hardly an effective response to a world that has long ago moved away from steam to propel growth.

In many organizations, we still rely on old practices because, like steam trains, they are familiar and we have an affection for doing things the way we have always done them. Steam trains have outlived their practical usefulness as a means of transport and many of our practices have outlived their relevance, but organizations often cling to them (Figure 2.2).

The old models of organizational design are at best inadequate and at worst failing. Currently we have a lack of imagination and a sunken-cost mindset in

FIGURE 2.2 *A steam train. Working in some old paradigms is like perfecting steam train technology – comforting but pointless.*

FIGURE 2.3 *Singapore is continually transforming.*

organizations that will damage their ability to be agile and ready for change. Singapore is a small nation state (721.5 sq. km.) with a population of over 5.5 million people situated in the most dynamic region on the globe. The Singapore government as an organization has been vigilant to ensure that it moves with postnormal times, not only reacting to but also anticipating change. Singapore continues to attempt and re-imagine transformation in a rapidly changing world (Figure 2.3).

Singapore re-imagining business as usual

Singapore has relied on its human capital to make it the modern prosperous success story it is today. At the heart of this success is not the ability to mine resources or create great wealth through growing commodities but rather the development of national wealth through building a modern service-orientated economy. The government have sensed, however, that to continue doing what they have always done will leave their citizens unprepared for a rapidly changing world. In 2012, Singapore was one of the first Asian nations to signal a move away from rote learning and a move towards prioritising creativity. The Minister for Education, Heng Swee Keat, argued that education should be 'less about content knowledge but more about how to process information … to allow students to discern truths from untruths, connect seemingly disparate dots, and create knowledge even as the context changes'.[14]

These changes demonstrate an imagination that many of our organizations and communities lack. While many of our governments (especially in the UK, US and Australia) 'double down' on testing and rote learning in a supposed aping of the Singaporean success, Singaporean education policy and practice has moved on. The old ways of surviving and thriving are being recognized as outmoded by agile savvy economies such as Singapore. In their case the reality of success a decade ago has not led to complacency but a re-imagining of what might make that society successful in the twenty-first century.

We must strive for the same re-imagining in our own communities and the organizations within them. Postnormality presents challenges to organizations to reconsider the old 'normalities'. It provides an opportunity for us to re-imagine what organizations could be in a 'post-fact' world where employees require the skills and understanding to confront the contradictions, chaos and complexities of the future. In Singapore's case, the emergent postnormalities have been incorporated into new national strategies that attempt to build the capacity for social and economic agility in the face of change.

What is postnormality and how does it affect organizations?

If we are moving into a state of contradictions, chaos and complexity there are profound implications for organizations. Before we examine these implications in depth we would like to explore exactly what postnormality looks like in practice. According to philosopher and futurist Ziauddin Sardar the postnormal age is 'characterised by uncertainty, rapid change, realignment of power, upheaval and chaotic behaviour'.[15] In other words, the normalities organizations once clung to are no longer reliable. In Sardar's view this is a moment of transition where the old ways seem outmoded and new ways seem unreliable, unimaginable or impossible. He argues that the combination of complexity, confusion and contradiction has fuelled a shift from normality to postnormality, sweeping away the institutions and understanding society has clung to for thousands of years and replacing them with uncertainty.

A recent example of this kind of widespread disruption emerged in the global financial crisis where chaos, complexity and contradiction reigned. While financial crises are not new, the rebalancing of labour and resource economics from the West to the East means that the 'debt and deficit' business as usual model has become vulnerable and open to question. Many of the entrenched practices taken for granted in our organizations that emerged in normal times have become potentially irrelevant. CEO and consultant, Gill Ringland argues that we are in for some difficult times as we adjust to postnormality: 'Global systems issues – such as environmental change, but also international law and finance, access to raw materials and the management of intellectual property – all require the rich nations to sacrifice some of their power. This combination of power rebalancing and an institutional vacuum implies that the next decade will be a turbulent one.'[16] While science and technology have driven economic growth in many economies, there has been a less welcome rise in the side effects of these technologies. As Marshall and Picou argue, 'these same advances tend to manufacture environmental problems that are increasingly complex, large-scale, and destructive'.[17] There is a paradoxical bind here. Society has become reliant on the network and market economies but their combined fruits are sometimes poisonous, such as pollution, deforestation, climate change and global financial crises. The first of Sardar's postnormal conditions is complexity.

Complexity

One of the most compelling demonstrations of postnormal complexity is the ongoing 'wars' on 'terrorism' whether they are state sanctioned or initiated by organizations such as Hamas or ISIS. These conflicts are responses to an abhorrent act such as a terror strike or a chemical weapons attack on civilian populations. There are, however, complex forces at work as the networked international community assesses the cost of action and/or non-action on the global community. Morality in these cases is shaped and driven at least in part by energy security and the economic pressures higher oil prices bring to bear on local economies. The networking and linking of these geopolitical and economic factors integrated with the rapid delivery of news coverage brings new complexities to bear on decision makers and creates heightened tensions for political leaders.

In one of the main theatres of the war on terror, Afghanistan, the Eisenhower Study Group[18] records the civilian death toll as 210,000 in addition to the 2,996 who were killed in the 9/11 attacks.[19] These wars on terror with their theatres in New York, London, Bali, Paris, Afghanistan and Iraq have taken an enormous toll in human life and human hope. These are complex, confusing and chaotic conflicts. In the face of these postnormal conflicts, how can individuals and communities untangle the issues and make clear and wise decisions? The attacks of 9/11 remain abhorrent, but do they justify the torture and civilian deaths that have been the legacy of the West's war on terror? This 'war' seems in some ways more complex than many others from our past. And perhaps this complexity is a contributing factor to Sardar's next condition: chaos.

Chaos

A new brand of chaos has become more prevalent in our mostly civil societies. In 2005 in Australia we saw the largest ever race riot being co-ordinated on mobile phones.[20] Racist anarchy reigned and the peaceful seaside Australian suburb of Cronulla exploded in the most extreme and chaotic partisan violence seen in years. In 2011 in the UK in Hackney, Brixton, Chingford, Bristol, Manchester, Birmingham and Liverpool chaotic riots also stained the landscape[21] and then again in the USA in Baltimore in 2015. These riots had the added feature of social media that propelled the suddenness and the ferocity of the chaos. As communications expert Stephanie Baker points out, riots in the UK are not novel but 'new social media played a key role in organizing the recent riots with smart phones giving those with access to these technologies the power to network socially and to incite collective disorder'.[22] Violent protest in the postnormal world is organized, co-ordinated and delivered through digitally networked crowds for the insatiable media audiences. These complexities and chaos invariably produce regular contradictions in the postnormal world.

Contradictions

Sardar's third condition of postnormality is contradictions. As he says, we now live in: 'A complex, networked world, with countless competing interests and ideologies, designs and desires, behaving chaotically, can do little more than throw up contradictions . . . It is the natural product of numerous antagonistic social and cultural networks jostling for dominance'.[23] A vivid example of this contradictory state is the mismatch between research evidence and public policy. There are frequent examples of scientific evidence (especially around global climate change) being ignored in the face of 'alternative facts'. We have seen recent examples in the UK in Brexit and in the US in the election of President Trump where scientific expertise became synonymous in political rhetoric, with elitism making evidence-based policy a distant fantasy. In these cases, fundamentally contradictory pieces of evidence become policy and practice. These contradictions have become so entrenched that often the practices go on largely unchallenged. Contradictory policy is allowed to stand because in postnormal times society seems to have drastically reduced its ability to discern or trust 'normal' sources of evidence.

Sardar's postnormal conditions (contradiction, complexity and chaos) provide a dramatic context for the changes that face our society and our organizations. There are also radical shifts emerging in the way we work and organize work.

Organizations and the future of work

In 2013, a team from Oxford university headed up by Karl Frey and Michael Osborne[24] undertook a study called: 'The future of employment: how susceptible are jobs to computerisation?'[25] In this research they investigated 702 different occupations to analyse and model how technology would change the kind of jobs we do now. They also examined the workforce impact of technology such as cloud computing, robotics, artificial intelligence (AI), automation and big data mining. They made some fascinating findings. They found that 47 per cent of workers in the US are currently at risk. In 2015, a report by the Committee for Economic Development Australia found a similar trend.[26] Critically, jobs that do not require social interaction and that have low levels of creativity are more likely to be replaced by automation and artificial intelligence.

What can organizations do to prepare themselves for this rapid change? Frey and Osborne make this finding: 'For workers to win the race, however, they will have to acquire *creative* and *social skills* [our emphasis]'.[27] These labour market economists found almost half the jobs that currently exist are likely to be eliminated within a decade or so. By the time a child who is five years old today turns sixteen, half of the jobs we are preparing her for will not be there according to this growing body of research. Perhaps this is a massive wake-up call. This is a call to action that does not only encourage, but demands we re-think how we educate and train our young people. It also questions the priorities we pursue in organizations. In this time of rapid change, it is critical that organizations build capacities like the 4Cs and build organizational effectiveness (see the Organizational Effectiveness Wheel, Chapter 3) to make them ready for rapid changes and unpredictable shifts. While organizations may not be able to imagine what the shifts are they can build the capacities to make their responses agile, wise and effective.

This research shows change is upon us and we need to act swiftly or our organizations may be doomed to irrelevance and obsolescence.

Changing organizations

In our view, our organizations and communities already have the raw materials for change. For instance, in our schools and universities we have able transformative educators who understand how critical changing structures and approaches in learning are for preparing students for an uncertain future. Our organizations are now used to 'disruptive' challenges and we have many examples in these chapters and elsewhere of organizations who respond to this challenge by acting wisely to re-imagine their practices.

In this book, we want to bridge the gap between rhetoric and reality. The reality is that organizations face perhaps some of the most difficult challenges since the industrial revolution. The rhetoric is clear: we need to change. Yet the how is often illusive. In our work with the 4Cs we see organizations who build capacities in creativity, critical reflection, communication and collaboration, effectively reshaping themselves for an uncertain future. If organizations are to respond to the big picture changes we know are emerging in job roles, society and our economy we need to transform our organizational systems to make the 4Cs central to the way we work. These are the capacities that Sardar (2010),[28] Osborne and Frey (2013)[29] and others argue will be crucial not only to survive but thrive in the mid to late twenty-first century.

Where to now? Transforming organizations through the 4Cs

Lego's near-death experience that opened this book in Chapter 1 uncovers a set of challenges for organizations. Like Nokia, Lego's 'business as usual' model had failed to deliver and in that vacuum fear had been the dominant transformation strategy. A gap emerged for Lego between doing business in normal times and entering a postnormal period. They survived by building capacities in the 4Cs to deliver transformational leadership, deep organizational learning and re-imagined practices. These capacities may not have mattered as much when we had 'normality' to cling to, but in the rapidly changing twenty-first century, incremental or trivial change may lead to irrelevance which ultimately leads to organizational failure. The interconnectedness of the modern postnormal world featuring complexity, chaos and contradiction demands new approaches to new challenges. In Chapter 9 we provide a coherence maker for transformation, the Transformation Tangle, that clarifies and provides structure for those contemplating transformation.

We need transformation for our organizations, our leaders, managers and employees, and ultimately our societies. We are arguing here for organizations to change in ways that make them unrecognizable from the old factory models of the past. We are imagining new leadership, processes and strategies that put the 4Cs at the centre of what we do and how we deliver. What we imagine is what we glimpse in the transformations we see in our work with organizations on a daily basis. We believe this change is not only possible but that it is essential to make organizations relevant to the needs of a changing and sometimes insecure world.

In the next chapter, we explore how we can prepare the ground for transformation to close the gap between rhetoric and reality. Chapter 3 discusses how moving from a 'business as usual' model to a 4Cs approach is achievable once the ground is prepared.

3

Preparing the ground: preconditions for transformation

Case study: Woolf Farming and Processing[1]

FIGURE 3.1 *Changing practices in agriculture means new thinking is required.*

The sun seems like an unlimited resource for farmers but the vagaries of weather, climate change and global markets mean they have to continually manage uncertainty. There is uncertainty in whether the rains will come, what produce they should grow and as a consequence, how they should develop their business as an organization. Stuart Woolf, CEO of Woolf Farming and Processing,[2] is a farmer and producer in sun-drenched California who in recent years has been dealing with drought and zero surface-water allocation. Woolf Farming and Processing is a family-owned three-generation business that proudly states: 'Our goal is to build an enduring family business upon the simple notion of feeding more people with fewer resources. We will achieve this through good stewardship, reinvestment and innovation.' Rather than growing the traditional rotational grain crops of the San Joaquin Valley, the Woolf family developed higher value speciality crops including almonds, tomatoes, pistachios and garlic. As a farming organization, they have a history of re-investment, developing infrastructure and innovation to successfully expand their operations, but they continue to be challenged by the uncertainty of the climate, weather and the allocation of water resources.

Whether it is the weather, the volatility of the stock market, the rapid change of technology, the dependence on global economics, the effects of government policy, the influence of geopolitical crises and changes in society etc., the case study of Woolf Farming and Processing highlights the uncertainty that all organizations face in postnormal times. All organizations have to meet that uncertainty continually if they want to remain relevant, sustainable and effective. But the Woolf farm has a conundrum. Despite past successful innovations in experimenting with crops and technologies to survive dry spells, and expanding into food processing and investments, the long-term drought and zero water allocation has taken them to a new tipping point. They are asking themselves; are rising temperatures and volatile weather the usual pattern of events for farming or are they dealing with a new climate norm? Should they continue with business as usual or should they continue transforming their business? Should they go into organic produce where the profit is potentially greater? Or should they invest in developing solar energy on their land? Should they drill more groundwater wells? Or should they advocate for the development of a water trading market for efficient water allocation? Or should they just sell the farm and begin again by investing in something more viable? At the end of the chapter, we will return to the Woolf farm, and see what they decided to do.

These strategic and structural questions for Woolf farm all have to be considered on their short-term and long-term merits and ultimately how they affect the vision of what the farm wants to be: a family-run business organization that continues to feed the world population in an economical and environmentally sustainable way. How Woolf Farming and Processing goes forward is a matter of how they continue to transform to meet uncertainty. To transform, however, requires organizations to 'prepare the ground' to allow for transformation to happen, just as a crop must have prepared and fertile ground to begin to grow. If the organizational groundwork is there to transform, Woolf Farming can make challenging decisions, learn from success and failure and be agile and adaptive to fulfil their vision.

Preparing the ground

This chapter examines what organizations 'need to be' to operate through the 4Cs (creativity, critical reflection, communication and collaboration) to facilitate and make possible transformation. Preparing the ground for transformation is for organizations to understand the key concepts that underpin a 4C approach. These key concepts involve a 4C approach to leadership and an emphasis on organizational learning that transforms mindsets. We use what we call 'coherence makers' to develop learning in 4C processes and transformation. We use 'paradoxical thinking' to develop an organization's capacity to learn and make wise decisions in anticipation of future events. Wisdom is the capacity to reason and make the best decisions for the common good of the organization as well as society more generally. Without the 4Cs and wisdom, an organization like Woolf Farming and Processing cannot transform to deal with uncertainty and do what is best for the greater good.

What then are the pre-conditions for organizations to have the capacity to learn and enact the 4Cs to make wise decisions and transform? We argue it begins with organizations reflecting honestly about themselves and knowing whether they have the pre-conditions for 4C transformation. Organizations can assess this knowledge of themselves through the lens of our coherence maker, the Leading Organizations Framework. Before exploring the pre-conditions of transformation, we have to examine why have we developed coherence makers, what are they and how do they work?

What are coherence makers?

We often explain that the 4C words creativity, critical thinking, communication and collaboration have become 'aerosol words'; they are sprayed around, they smell pleasant but quickly vaporize into nothing (Figure 3.2). Perhaps due to their overuse the 4Cs as concepts have lost their meaning. We develop coherence makers to illuminate a structural meaning for organizations for concepts and ideas that are sometimes elusive. In this book, we have developed the following coherence makers:

- Leading Organizations Framework (Chapter 3)
- Organizational Effectiveness Wheel (Chapter 4)
- Deeper Learning Diamond (Chapter 4)
- Transformation Tangle (Chapter 9).

FIGURE 3.2 *'Aerosol words' vanish when you try and get hold of them.*

To learn and develop processes in the 4Cs we have developed coherence makers for creativity, critical reflection, communication and collaboration (Figure 3.3). They are the:

- Creativity Cascade (Chapter 5)

- Critical Reflection Crucible (Chapter 6)

- Communication Crystal (Chapter 7) and

- Collaboration Circles (Chapter 8).

Our coherence makers aim to make tangible the 'aerosol words' and 'aerosol concepts' and elaborate these processes (including the 4Cs) as complex but learnable to close the gap between rhetoric and reality.

So how do coherence makers work? Coherence makers are schemas that give clarity and order to complex concepts. The paradox of a coherence maker is that in its simplicity to make concepts clear, it should also open up hidden depths in

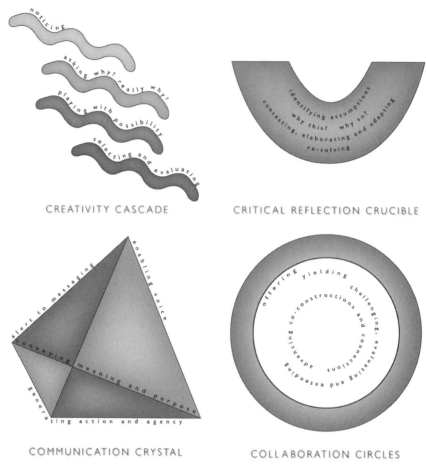

CREATIVITY CASCADE   CRITICAL REFLECTION CRUCIBLE

COMMUNICATION CRYSTAL   COLLABORATION CIRCLES

FIGURE 3.3 *The coherence makers for creativity, critical reflection, communication and collaboration.*

those concepts to ever-greater complexity. For instance, physics equations are coherence makers, as they are simple in design but complex in concept. The simple algebraic formula $E = mc^2$ (energy = mass × speed of light squared) for example is seemingly simple but it explains a complex and profound relationship between energy and matter. While our coherence makers are not equations, nor as profound, they attempt to reveal and address the complexity of concepts and processes like the 4Cs through simplicity. Coherence makers open out and deepen understanding rather than close and limit thinking. In their simplicity they make learning accessible but they should also challenge. They should not 'explain' everything so there is nothing to question and wonder at. Howard Gardner argues in *Five Minds for the Future*[3] that coherence or synthesis as a means to make connections to 'everything' must not paralyse the critical mind. For example the 4C coherence makers encourage an 'attitude of the mind' that supports as well as challenges a way of doing things. The 4Cs frame our approach, as demonstrated by our first coherence maker, the Leading Organizations Framework that we use to explain the significant pre-conditions (and continually evolving conditions) that support transformation.

The Leading Organizations Framework

To explain how we conceive leadership and 4C transformation in organizations we have developed a coherence maker that is demonstrated in Figure 3.4. What you will notice about this diagram is that leadership sits at the centre with the 4Cs arrayed around the term (leading organizations). We consider the 4Cs as components of effective leadership. There is no set sequence for these 4C components to occur. The smaller intersecting circles in Figure 3.4 indicate the components that we consider critical to organizations and transformation. The use of the Venn diagram suggests that the 4Cs are integrated into all facets of leadership: the vision, culture, structure, strategy and integration, collaborative partnerships, learning and evaluation. These are obviously not the only components of change, but they are from our experience the key components that are the most challenging and therefore critical to successful transformation.

We also use these leadership components to examine whether certain pre-conditions are in place for transformation. Each component has a question that leadership must assess of their organization and of themselves, and these are:

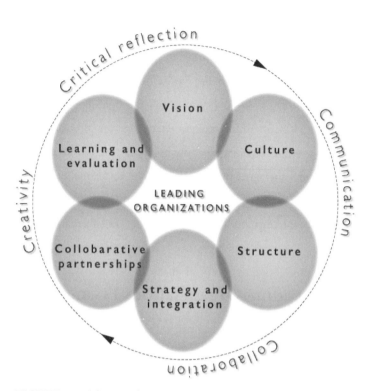

FIGURE 3.4 *The Leading Organizations Framework in the 4C approach.*

Vision: Is leadership fully engaged in 4C transformation of the organization?

Culture: Is there a critical mass of willing and able members of the organization ready to engage in 4C transformation?

Structure: Are there structures to support 4C transformation?

Strategy and Integration: Can the strategic thinking of the organization be integrated with 4C transformation?

Collaborative partnerships: Are there collaborations that can support and challenge 4C transformation in the organization?

Learning and evaluation: Will learning and evaluation support 4C transformation?

We discuss how these components and questions clarify and establish what is needed in the pre-conditions for transformation. The first component in our model for 4C transformational leadership is the much-derided term, vision.

Vision: Is leadership fully engaged in 4C transformation of the organization?

The term vision is perhaps so overused that it has begun to lose its meaning, but for leading change it is possibly the most critical starting point. Vision is encapsulated by the Roman politician and philosopher Cicero, who said: 'Let us not go over the old ground, let us rather prepare for what is to come.' A vision of where an organization wants to go focuses the organization to achieve that vision.[4] Having a vision is crucial to organizational success but it alone does not create success. Too often organizations have vision statements that are just that, statements. The 'talk' of vision does not necessarily mean the 'walk' towards that vision. In some ways the disconnection between talking and walking is why vision has become so meaningless as a term. In Chapter 1 we refer to this disconnection as the rhetoric reality gap. It is relatively easy to state a vision but exponentially more difficult to implement. That leadership must be fully engaged in the vision of 4C transformation sounds too obvious. Leadership and vision should go together but in our experience, leaders can sometimes talk the vision but do not necessarily *lead* organizations towards that vision. It is not just politicians who find it easy to have visionary policies in an election campaign and then, in the reality of governing, find it difficult to implement those policies.

A vision is an aspiration for an organization but crucially it does not tell you the processes to achieve that vision. The why, what and how of 4C transformation is the focus of this book and in our pre-conditions, leaders must be fully invested in leading that process. If leadership outsources the 4C approach to others to learn, they do not understand that the 4Cs must be imbedded in every aspect of organizational life, including leadership. If leadership is not involved in 4C transformation, it is difficult for them to lead something they do not understand, practice or model. In short, if there is not time, energy or commitment for leadership to lead 4C transformation, the organization cannot be transformed.

For instance, in an educational organization we worked with recently, leaders were big on the vision and rhetoric of being future focused and transformational, so we gave support to a team to imbed the 4Cs in their work, but the leaders themselves did not have time to engage with 4C transformational practices. By not having time, they did not see the 4Cs as relevant to their managing and leading the organization, but they were happy for others to learn. In time the 4C team were transforming their teaching practice and gaining success in student learning. Leadership was supportive of the gains but had no understanding of why, what and how the changes happened. They stood on the outside looking in rather than being in the middle of the change. Gradually two very distinct, disconnected cultures began to operate in the organization – a '4C way of doing things' and a 'non 4C way of doing things'. In the end, the 4C team perceived a lack of engagement and understanding from leadership, and began to feel constricted in expanding their work despite their success. As a result, members of the staff of the school on the 4C team left the educational organization. This example illustrates not only the necessity for leadership to walk the talk; it also demonstrates how a 4Cs approach impacts an organization's culture. Culture also has a role in the pre-conditions for transformation.

Culture: Is there a critical mass of willing and able members of the organization ready to engage in 4C transformation?

Strategy, structure and vision are critical to begin the process of change but a shift in culture is necessary for that change to be sustained. And culture cannot be changed overnight. It is deeply embedded in the foundations of an organization. Culture is the deep-rooted assumptions and beliefs that give rise to the climate of attitudes and behaviours.[5] You have to read the climate or observable reality of an organization to begin to understand and get a feel for the underpinning culture. For instance, here are two climates: (a) an upbeat atmosphere where people generate ideas with each other, and (b) an atmosphere where certain topics are avoided. In (a), the observable upbeat climate is underpinned by a cultural belief that new ideas are valued and invigorate an organization (for example, Lego). In (b), the cultural belief is that certain topics dangerously undermine the staff's commitment to the prescribed aims of an organization (such as Nokia).

The assumptions that shape culture work invisibly and below the surface.[6] Culture hides behind the climate of slick office designs, high-minded mission statements, website slogans, dress codes, the way meetings are run, the way ideas are generated, and the narratives constructed about an organization. Because assumptions and beliefs that uphold culture are complex and invisible, they often feel impenetrable and resistant to change. But transformation involves a cultural change as Global Leadership director Michael Fullan argues, 'Structure does make a difference, but it is not the main point in achieving success. Transforming culture – changing the way we do things around here – is the main point, it is a particular kind of reculturing for which we strive.'[7]

4C transformation is a development of culture that values the fruits and flourishing of creativity, critical reflection, communication and collaboration. It is therefore a pre-condition to ask, are there enough organizational members (and leadership) ready to engage with 4C transformation to affect cultural change? We call this group of organizational members a critical mass of the willing and able, and it is with them that leadership can begin or develop a 4C cultural shift. In our experience the leadership team needs a group of collaborators in the organization who are open to being the early adopters of 4C processes. This group of early adopters will create a collaborative culture that builds trust to experiment with and develop 4C processes. The critical mass of the willing and able are mindfully chosen by leadership as key change agents that will influence the organizational climate and affect cultural change over time.

Culture is, however, only one facet of an organization's DNA. The way an organization is organized or structured is symptomatic of culture, but at the same time structures shape culture, and so structures too lay the groundwork for 4C transformation.

Structure: Are there structures to support 4C transformation?

Structures are how we organize people, work and time to best achieve what is valued in an organization. Structures can be hierarchies, roles and responsibilities, workflow and priorities, rules and regulations, processes and procedures, and the physical or virtual environment. Structures in an organization should be dependent on what we think optimises human flourishing not just functioning, but this is not always the case. Structures are necessary for effective organization but an over-emphasis on them can inundate organizations and lead to weakening the delivery of their core business.[8]

Organizations can be over-consumed by building structures and correct procedures to ensure they have 'ticked all the boxes'. Being consumed by structures is what bureaucracies are pilloried for, and this is satirized in the classic BBC TV series, *Yes, Prime Minister*. The following exchange is an example of being so consumed by structure it becomes a strategy:

> Bernard Woolley: What if the Prime Minister insists we help them?
> Sir Humphrey Appleby: Then we follow the four-stage strategy.
> Bernard Woolley: What's that?
> Sir Richard Wharton: Standard Foreign Office response in a time of crisis
> Sir Richard Wharton: In stage one we say nothing is going to happen.

Sir Humphrey Appleby: Stage two, we say something may be about to happen, but we should do nothing about it.

Sir Richard Wharton: In stage three, we say that maybe we should do something about it, but there's nothing we 'can' do.

Sir Humphrey Appleby: Stage four, we say maybe there was something we could have done, but it's too late now[9].

Ironically the focus on structures can override any real work being done and the structures themselves become an organizational fetish. As a fetish, structures themselves can supplant the real work of an organization. In our *Yes, Prime Minister* example, the Foreign Office is about implementing procedure, not actually doing anything in a time of crisis. An example from a financial institution arises when bankers' performance bonuses are based on the numbers of new accounts, and so opening new accounts becomes an organizational fetish, rather than the core work of managing finances and servicing customers. In education, it is when an audit paperwork culture of meeting compliance goals becomes the main focus of teachers, rather than the actual learning in classrooms. Or in a philanthropic organization, the focus and energy is in structures to apply for funding grants, and so gaining grants becomes the organization's work, not organizing support for those in need.

Structures too can become superficial or rigid, and constrain what is possible. Authors, Alvesson and Spicer argue:

Formal structures, rules and routines can be a source of significant stupidity in organizations. They are necessary, but many organizations overdo them. Structures are often mistaken for guarantees of quality, productivity and reliability. Far-reaching division of labour encourages tunnel vision and box-ticking. Most people have a limited overview and do not make much effort to carefully look behind surface structures.[10]

Critical reflection as one of the 4Cs is a capability to look past surface structures and consider deeper and wider implications of the organization's work. Rather than tunnel vision, critical reflection aims to open up thinking and question assumptions, and see potential connections in the broader context of the organization. Critical reflection then requires time and space in organizational structures and priorities to overcome tunnel vision and box-ticking.

The 4Cs are processes that influence the nature of structures. Collaboration, for example, invites more permeable structures in organizations, and creativity is born from more self-organizing and emergent structures. In our view, the right ideas are found in the right structures. In the preconditions for 4C transformation there must be structures that allow time and space for people to learn deeply and reflect on the application of 4C learning. A one off 'training' day in 4Cs processes, while a good place to start, will not deepen and transform working practice. The 4Cs are mindset processes and they require a commitment of time and energy to understand, learn and develop. This can only happen if there are flexible and adaptive structures in place to support this. Structures like vision and culture can only be developed if there is strategic thinking and integration in an organization.

Strategy and Integration: Can the strategic thinking of the organization be integrated with 4C transformation?

In our view the 'heavy lifting' occurs when organizational leadership face the sometimes daunting task of putting visions and structures into practice. Strategic thinking is noticing the issues, asking the why questions and playing with the possibilities to find the pathways, bridges and highways to move towards a desired future. But like structures, 4C processes do not lend themselves to rigid strategies, plans and implementation that are carefully controlled and managed. The 4C's: creativity, critical reflection, communication and collaboration promote strategic thinking that is flexible, adaptive and emergent.

A 4C approach to strategic thinking is more in keeping with Mintzberg's notion of 'adhocracy'.[11] Adhocracy is not makeshift or reactive strategy, it still involves foresight and planning but it is not fixed. It is strategic thinking that has a sense of direction but is open and responsive to the unpredictable, the uncertain and the complex, so it cannot be an absolute blueprint for a determined direction. Instead the strategic direction is continually being modified, critically reflected upon and generated as a collaborative co-construction. We argue strategic thinking is strengthened when creative and adaptive processes are integrated fundamentally in the collective thinking of an organization. But integrating collective thinking across an organization does not happen overnight.

Integration is the skill of knowing how and when and what scale to implement strategies and with whom. Any transformation requires a layering and a balancing across complex areas of an organization. Strategy and integration is similar to 'playing chess in three dimensions'; integration is the co-ordination and layering of strategies to create a coherent and collaborative process of change across the organization to inspire confidence and trust in the strategic process and direction being undertaken. There are different and differentiated starting points for all members of an organization in the process of learning and change. A 'one-size fits all' splash of 4C learning will not work in a deep, sustained and integrated way. However, as a precondition for transformation, the 4Cs have to be integrated with the organization's strategic direction. Like strategy and integration, collaborative partnerships can also support and challenge 4C transformation.

Collaborative partnerships: Are there collaborations that can support and challenge 4C transformation in the organization?

Collaborative partnerships are a rich source for opening up and integrating new ways of thinking and learning in organizations. Collaborations release organizations from being trapped in their own history. For instance, the collaboration between Mercedes and Swatch led to the Smart Car; the collaboration of the two major airline alliances, One World and Star Alliance led to clever networking; the Laser Interferometer Gravitational-Wave Observatory (LIGO) collaboration of 1,000 scientists from fifteen countries led to a large-scale physics experiment and the detection of cosmic gravitational waves; the theatre company Ex Machina's collaborative partnerships with architects, scientists, historians and technicians led to innovative multi-disciplinary performances; the collaboration between Johns Hopkins Medicine and grassroots community organizations led to better health and social outcomes for patients (see Chapter 8). Collaborations trigger new insights and generate new thinking because these partnerships traverse the knowledge boundaries of the organization.[12] It sounds like something all organizations would be involved with, but although a dynamic source for insight and growth, many organizations view collaborations with scepticism or fear. Collaboration may mean access to valuable information and know how, and losing the competitive advantage.

Collaborations are a paradoxical relationship to navigate. To work across boundaries requires understanding the ways of a particular organization, and at the same time the transgression of boundaries should challenge the organization's thinking. Boundary crossing necessitates trust and confidence in the relationships and shared endeavour that binds the collaboration. Collaboration is a complex, learnt and transparent process that involves a sharing of knowledge that is mutually beneficial to all collaborators whether they are partnerships, clients, customers, suppliers, retailers, agencies, universities or consultants.

To prepare the ground for transformation, collaborative partnerships can work to support and challenge the learning and growth of 4C practice. The collaboration, however, should be a co-construction that is aware of the trust, respect, communication and understanding that is needed to traverse mutual boundaries to develop new ideas. We are partners with organizations, working with them in how to learn and develop the 4Cs in their particular context. It has to be a partnership that is a 'true' collaboration and a shared endeavour between our organization and theirs. It is through the mutuality of collaborative partnerships that learning and evaluation can generate new ideas and progress.

Learning and evaluation: Will learning and evaluation support 4C transformation?

Too often in organizations, being busy and taking action is mistaken for progress. Busy work is operational activity that keeps organizations distracted from reflecting about and genuinely addressing whether an organization is really making progress. In a business, the busy work can be dealing with clients, in law it can be dealing with litigation, in health it can be dealing with patients, but the busy, operational work can prevent evaluation and learning about how to transform the client service, legal system and health providers to be more effective and equitable. Busy work keeps us occupied and believing the work we do is productive, however, we cannot know the work is productive unless we stop being reactive to, and too busy with, day-to-day operations. Being busy maintains the status-quo and deprioritises the significance of how to progress the effectiveness and transformation of the organization's operations.

Progress through innovation and transformation must be meaningful; it must change the way an organization sees and does things, and add value for the greater good. Progress does not happen without learning and evaluation, and transformation does not happen without wisdom. This is 'wise action' or *praxis* and it involves learning and 'knowing why, how, and when to adapt to the environment and why, how and when to change it.'[13] 4C transformation and progress should manifest as praxis – continual learning through reflection, dialogue and practice.

We argue that organizations must be learning communities deep in their culture. This develops the capacity of knowing what, why and how to solve problems and develop new possibilities, to adapt and transform. Learning in creativity, critical reflection, communication and collaboration in organizations has to be applied *insitu* to authentic work practices; it has to be deeper learning or generative learning.[14] We discuss this in greater detail in Chapter 4, but in essence deeper or generative learning is learning that can be transferred and adapted to new and changing situations. Learning deeply is essential to developing the 4Cs, and of course the 4Cs are integral to learning deeply and generating on-going learning. The 4Cs cannot be implemented; they can only be learnt.

As organizations lay the groundwork, they must ask: Will learning and evaluation support 4C transformation in the organization? To engage deeply with transformation means learning is a continuing inquiry that challenges and critically evaluates ideas, decisions and actions in the 4C approach itself. If learning and evaluation do not continue to inform the 4Cs in an organization, it is no longer a creative, critically reflective, communicative and collaborative organization. Learning and evaluation feeds the growth and effectiveness of an organization to transform.

Based on learning and evaluation, Woolf Farming and Processing can generate ideas, consider their options (solar energy production, water allocation advocacy, technology for water usage efficiency or even selling the farm) and decide what steps to take next.

Effective learning should never stop in an organization. Humans have the capacity to learn throughout their lives, and the more that is understood about the neuroplasticity or re-wiring capability of the adult brain, the more neuroscientists realize that human brain architecture can be constantly developed by the learning environment, conditions and culture of an organization. Science writer, Moheb Costandi explains brain plasticity:

> Far from being fixed, the brain is a highly dynamic structure, which undergoes significant change not only as it develops but also throughout

the entire lifespan. Neuroplasticity simply means change in the nervous system, and is a collective term for all the processes that that change the structure and function of the brain. Brains evolved to respond and adapt to the environment, and so neuroplasticity is an intrinsic property of nervous tissue, which occurs at all levels of organization, from the genetic to the behavioural.[15]

Adult brains can change to adapt to environments and determine the best course of action, particularly in organizations with effective 4C learning cultures. In preparing the ground then, it is essential for organizations to understand how a 4C approach develops learning, thinking and transformation. Central to the 4Cs approach is understanding 4C processes, essentially as learning that is a change or transformation of an individual's mindset. This is what transformation in an organization is really all about.

How do we learn to transform mindsets?

Jack Mezirow is a leading thinker in adult education and transformative learning. Mezirow argues that learning is transformational when it is a comprehensive shift in how we see ourselves; it involves a recalibration of personality and identity. Transformational learning is the result of challenges or a crisis-like situation that make it necessary to change. It is 'both profound and extensive, it demands a lot of mental energy and when accomplished it can often be experienced physically, typically as a feeling of relief or relaxation.'[16] Transformation in the 4Cs approach is charged both emotionally and mentally because it involves a complete change in a person's 'frame of reference'. Frames of reference are pre-conceptions that define our life view and they become our habitual viewpoint and line of action unless we reflect critically on our own and others' assumptions.

For example, a recent study[17] looked at gender equality in an organization where women are under-represented in upper management and make up only 20 per cent of the most senior roles. A persistent argument (assumption) is that this occurs because of behavioural differences between men and women. The study had a number of hypotheses about why women were not in senior positions. Perhaps women had fewer mentors, or less face-to-face time with managers, or were not as proactive talking to senior managers. To test these assumptions, they used digital communication data and sociometric badges[18] with sensors that tracked person-to-person communication which meant measuring patterns of movements, proximity to others, volume and tone of voice, who talks to whom, where people communicate, and who dominates conversations.

When they analysed the data they found no difference between the behaviour of men and women in their communication with senior management. Women had the same number of contacts as men, they spent as much time with senior leadership, and they allocated their time similarly to men in the same role. If the behaviours are the same, what explains the differences in promotion rates between men and women in the company? The difference was due not to the behaviour of the women but to how they were treated. The data implied that gender differences may lie not in how women act but in how people perceive their actions. This suggests that the difference in promotion rates is caused by bias. Bias is when two groups of people act identically but one group is perceived differently. This study demonstrates how fixed and hidden a frame of reference (bias) can be. To change the original assumption (that gender inequality is behavioural) and to change a habitual frame of reference of bias (a hidden perceptual prejudice) requires critical reflection and learning to transform a mindset.

When ideas fail to fit our pre-conceptions we have a strong inclination to reject them and label them as irrelevant, undoable, fanciful, nonsense or mistaken. For instance, when we discuss the possibilities of creativity, critical reflection, communication or collaboration learning in organizations we sometimes hear pre-conceived responses such as, 'we haven't got time for those things, we have too much work to do', or 'the corporate approach is competitive, it doesn't really do collaboration', or 'not everyone wants to think in an organization, we as leaders have to do the thinking for them', or 'our work isn't that creative'. Instead, transformative learners move towards a frame of reference that is open yet discriminating, responsive to experience yet self-reflective.[19] Transformation means having a changed perspective and attitude, and changing your actions because of that. Transformative learners develop a disposition that is more critically reflective of their own assumptions and those of others. Rather than continuing established patterns of default thinking or sometimes 'non-thinking', transformative learners make decisions and carry out actions based on their transformed insights.[20]

4C learning and processes in organizations should be experiences that help individuals and organizations see things differently and act on things differently in a profound way. 4C learning is a mindset change that shifts our frames of reference; it is not simply an additional skill adding to what we already know. To illustrate how the 4Cs are a way of thinking that shifts our frames of reference and not merely the training of skills, we examine the role of paradoxes in 4C thinking and reasoning.

What is the role of paradoxes?

Paradoxes are two things that exist at the same time, but the two things totally contradict or seemingly cancel each other out. They seem nonsensical but the reality is they can exist together. The ancient philosopher Socrates' famous paradox, All I know is that I know nothing, indicates that knowing and knowing nothing simultaneously exist and can complement each other in their contradiction. It ends up being not one way or the other, but two contradictions working with each other. This relationship between the contradictions gives rise to a tension or dynamic that can generate a truth or a discovery. Philosophers, scientists, artists and mathematicians through time continue to use paradoxes to make sense of the complex to discover a truth. In *The Picture of Dorian Gray* Oscar Wilde wrote, 'The way of paradoxes is the way of truth. To test reality we must see it on the tight-rope.'

Paradoxical thinking uses the tightrope between contradictions to test ideas and explore the complex. The concept of coherence makers discussed previously in this chapter bring 'order' to understanding the complex; paradoxes are on the other hand a way to explore the 'disorder' of the complex. By disorder we mean looking at multiple perspectives and possibilities in situations that are often confusing, non-linear and challenging. This is referred to as paradoxical wisdom and Rodrigues, Pina e Cunha, Rego and Clegg[21] argue it is fundamental to developing wise leadership, management and work in an organization:

Paradoxical wisdom involves the contemplation of multiple events whether they are related or not, rather than a logic of cause and effect. It requires openness to new possibilities, willingness to learn and be challenged. Additionally, it implies the courage to go against the status quo and the confidence to move between poles without the fear of appearing incoherent or weak. Multiple perspectives increase complexity, but also raise the chance of breakthroughs. More importantly, it envisions shared values and acting for the common good which generates more sustainable outcomes.[22]

We argue that exploring the tension of contradictions in paradoxes deepens learning, leadership and wisdom in 4C thinking. In particular we focus on the following paradoxes to explore complexity and the 4Cs in organizations:

1 Structure and improvisation (in creativity).

2 Comfort and challenge (in critical reflection).

3 Decisive and consultative leadership (in collaboration).

4 Ambiguity and clarity (in communication).

The structure and improvisation paradox (in creativity)

Structure refers to the need for establishing ordered organizational efficiency and effectiveness in work practices and workflow. Structures have already been discussed in the chapter as frameworks that promote clarity and smooth operations within organizations. Improvisation, on the other hand, refers to a looseness or lack of structure that allows for spontaneity and the unexpected. Improvisation is generated by a group of people engaged in complex and unpredictable interactions. From the spontaneity and unpredictability of improvisation possibilities are played with and new ideas are created and this is explained as *creative emergence*.[23]

The way structures work in organizations often encourage predictable interactions between people. Structure and improvisation can appear to contradict and negate each other. However, paradoxical thinking allows improvisation and structure not to be considered in opposition but to be explored as a positive and dynamic state of tension. How organizations move between structure and improvisation can unlock how organizations understand complexity and generate creativity. Bilton and Cummings (2014) argue: 'Organizations have to be *loose* enough to allow for new ideas and inputs to be released and thus regenerate them, whilst at the same time being *controlled* enough to draw these diverse inputs into a common direction'.[24] IDEO is a design company we discuss in Chapter 7, and they are an organization that 'values strong ideas that are loosely held'. Here IDEO describes the structure (frameworks) and improvisation (brainstorming) that nurtures their creativity:

> To aid in the process of concepting, designers sought frameworks that distilled the behavioural patterns and themes they observed in the field. Once they created a framework, they stress-tested it by considering it from the perspectives of multiple customers. This assisted their brainstorming and testing of a wide array of possible solutions. However, the process was highly iterative, as designers moved between frameworks and brainstorming.[25]

The comfort and challenge paradox (in critical reflection)

The paradox between comfort and challenge impacts and defines the nature of learning in an organization. There is comfort in what is known, and there is a discomfort in not knowing and being challenged by the unknown. Comfort with the known can lead organizations to exploit and refine what they know and do well. Comfort with the known is attractive as it inspires confidence, ease and success in competency and excellence. But comfort can also be perfecting a routine of institutionalized learning that does not question, re-imagine and learn by challenging and exploring what is out there *to be* known.[26]

On the tightrope of this paradox are balanced the *comfort of certainty* and the *challenge of uncertainty*. There is often fear in the uncertainty of challenge and it requires being confident and open to unlearning default assumptions and open to learning from experience and failure. The paradox of comfort and challenge supports critical reflection and the development of wisdom. Wisdom is inherent in being comfortable with uncertainty and questioning what we assume to be certain. We learn wisdom by both knowing and doubting, and respecting what is known and what is unknown. As Rodrigues and colleagues argue: 'The need for a continuous sense of development by learning is characteristic of *wise people* that embrace the complexity of the world, persistently seeking new challenges to stretch their capabilities to be aware of the paradox of excellence or competency traps. They oscillate between comfort (what is known) and challenge (what is out there to be known).'[27]

The decisive and consultative leadership paradox (in collaboration)

In ever-growing globalization, the GLOBE leadership project[28] provides some insights into organizational leadership across societies and cultures. In their comprehensive study, they identified six global leadership styles and found that two styles are universally endorsed across countries and cultures. These two styles are charismatic/values-based leadership and team-oriented leadership.

Charismatic/values-based leaders lead with vision, inspiration and self-sacrifice and operate decisively and with integrity. Leaders who are team-oriented are collaborative, diplomatic, caring of others and administratively competent. Interestingly, there is somewhat of a paradox in these two styles. How can a leader be both independently decisive and collaboratively consultative? Does not collaboration and consultation interfere with a determined and decisive leader? Once again it is in the tension of the paradox of being both decisive and consultative that we argue the power of true collaborative and transformational leadership resides. Collaboration as we argue in Chapter 8 is not defined by consensus or co-operation. Collaboration is something far more difficult but far more effective and sustainable in making organizations dynamic and successful. Collaboration taps into the genius of the individuals in the group, rather than the sole genius of an individual. The sole genius of the individual is a misnomer as many have argued.[29] For example, Steve Jobs can credit the collaborative genius of working with Steve Wozniak in the development of Apple computers. Steve Jobs is a great example of a leader who became charismatic and dynamic as an individual, and at the same time a superb collaborator with people with whom he respected and trusted. He may not have started out this way, but he grew into a masterfully decisive yet consultative leader. This is what Steve Wozniak said about Jobs even in his early years:

> He would directly confront people and almost call them idiots ... But you know what? When they confronted him back and told him why they were right in understandable forms, he was just testing and learning, and he would respect those people and give them high privileges in the company. That was one thing he did respect – someone who believed

enough in their own ideas to speak for him, not just shut up and be shy around him.[30]

In this we see the beginnings of a collaborative approach that is clear and decisive but also recognizes diverse ideas and thinking can be harnessed to challenge, evaluate and extend leadership's thinking and decision making. Decisive yet consultative leadership is underpinned by our paradoxical understanding of collaboration in the 4Cs approach. The 'genius' of individual diverse thinking is key to the construction of the collective genius of group collaboration. In our concept of collaboration, identity is part individual agency and part group agency, and the paradox is in creating a 'liminal or transitional space' that fuses both. Individual agency gives rise to group agency and vice versa. Leadership that can tap and exploit this paradox can lead the continual dynamic of 4C transformation.

The ambiguity and clarity paradox (in communication)

Being both clear and ambiguous sounds like you are speaking 'spin' or 'weasel words' to obfuscate the truth and really say nothing. Sir Humphrey Appleby, the civil servant in *Yes, Prime Minister*, was famous for this, as the following exchange indicates:[31]

> Sir Humphrey Appleby: The identity of the official whose alleged responsibility for this hypothetical oversight has been the subject of recent discussion is not shrouded in quite such impenetrable obscurity as certain previous disclosures may have led you to assume, but, not to put too fine a point on it, the individual in question is, it may surprise you to learn, one whom your present interlocutor is in the habit of defining by means of the perpendicular pronoun.
>
> James Hacker: I beg your pardon?
>
> Sir Humphrey Appleby: It was . . . I.

Circumlocution and obfuscation is not what we mean by the combining of ambiguity and clarity. Clarity is a necessity if you want to convey a message as a two-way or multiple exchange between people. Clarity suggests you want to get across exactly what you mean without being cloudy, confusing, misleading or duplicitous. Integrity is at the heart of clear communication in the 4Cs approach. George Orwell argued; 'The great enemy of clear language is insincerity. When there is a gap between one's real and one's declared aims, one turns as it were instinctively to long words and exhausted idioms, like a cuttlefish spurting out ink.'[32]

Being clear does not mean being simplistic, superficial or brief. Significantly, clarity serves to better communicate the complex, the deep, the trustworthy, the wise and the profound. So how can clarity work with ambiguity? Ambiguity is more than one interpretation of something and can create a state of uncertainty in understanding. The sense of inexactitude in ambiguity would suggest a lack of clarity in communicating and understanding. In fact, ambiguity is usually at the heart of what is complex, deep, trustworthy, wise and profound. Let's use Escher's lithograph 'Order and Chaos' (1950) (Figure 3.5) as a beautiful example of communication that is both paradoxically ambiguous and clear at the same time. In the lithograph chaos as represented by broken objects is reflected in the perfect order of the crystal. Both order and chaos as represented by Escher is meticulously drawn, there is order in the drawing of the chaos. But at the same time the order of the drawn crystal is disrupted by the chaos surrounding it. Is Escher suggesting a connection between order and chaos?

The ambiguity of the message in Escher's lithograph means it is open to interpretation, but at the same time it quite clearly expresses something complex and profound. The paradox of clarity and ambiguity in communication is an honest and deeper way of dealing with, expressing and resolving the realness of uncertainty and equivocation in the way the world works. Clarity is to constantly try to make sense of the world through order, but the chaotic

FIGURE 3.5 *M.C Escher's 'Order and Chaos'*

principles of the universe and our own world in a state of postnormality creates ambiguity and complexity. In essence, it is looking for and finding clarity from a multitude of angles.

Paradoxical thinking

Tolerating ambiguity and uncertainty is an essential ingredient in developing creativity and wisdom. This is what creativity and wisdom scholar Robert Sternberg has to say about it:

> People often like things to be in black and white. They like to think a country is good or bad (ally or enemy) or that a given idea in education works or

does not work. The problem is that there are a lot of grays in creative work, just as there are when one invests in a stock whose value may or may not go up. Many stocks are low-valued. The ambiguities arise as to which will go up, when they will go up, and, even, for some individuals, what they can do to make them go up.[33]

The paradoxes we explore in the 4C approach are not intellectual brainteasers or conceptual gymnastics that bear no relationship with everyday practice. They do not paralyse thinking and work practices. They are a way of thinking that opens up organizations to continually develop creative and wiser solutions and ideas. Paradoxical thinking involves a relationship between uncertainties that can be described as dynamic stability.[34] It is the ability to understand and work with, and make sense of contradiction. Seeking out contradictions is more than recognizing the grey between the black and white; it is seeing the colours across the spectrum. By seeing more of the 'light', more successful and wiser decisions will be made, and better ideas will be generated.

4C processes are about thinking and acting. The 4Cs are not a programme, procedure or protocol, they are a philosophy, approach and mindset that can change an organization's culture. Human brains are plastic, they are malleable for growth with new learning, and to pruning back by accumulated unlearning and habitual assumptions that hide behind the way things have always been done. Learning that is transformative is to see things anew, to see the familiar as strange and to imagine and act on possibility. The 4C approach is an experience and an environment that has the capacity to change an individual's and an organization's frame of reference. It is a frame of reference that seeks out learning in creativity, critical reflection, communication and collaboration to meet, anticipate and create change. It is to be adaptive and agile to pursue and grow human flourishing; it is to transform an organization through wise action (*praxis*).

The case study of Woolf Farming and Processing that began this chapter reflects an organization dealing with the uncertainty of changing times and circumstances. Through practical reasoning and playing with possibility they continue to use new technology for greater farming efficiencies (particularly water efficiencies), they have invested in solar energy generation on the farm, they are considering how to convert agricultural waste into usable energy, they are actively campaigning for competitive water allocation reform in California and have developed a community garden that produces food for families hit by the lack of water. Woolf Farming and Processing's actions are wise, for they go beyond self-interest and self-aggrandisement, and serve the greater community in many ways.

According to business academic Bernard McKenna, wisdom is a philosophical orientation to the world that involves the physical, the ethical and the logical. Wisdom 'is embodied in our disposition to act in certain ways to produce that which is good. Although based on deep self-awareness, heedfulness of the other, worldly understanding and cognitively complex reasoning, wise action ultimately becomes embodied, habitual and resilient.'[35] As an organization, Woolf Farming and Processing embodies these attributes, and this book argues that the 4Cs and transformation must embody wise action (*praxis*) too.

Not all organizations are ready for transformation, and not all organizations want transformation. The ground is fertile when an organization sees learning and transformation through the 4Cs as a long-term investment and not a short-term 'silver bullet'. Preparing the ground is understanding that the 4Cs should permeate every aspect of an organization's vision, culture, structure, strategy and integration, collaborative partnerships, learning and evaluation. It is in knowing that transforming an organization is to transform mindsets through deeper organizational learning and thinking processes and through culture. 4C transformation is challenge and it is change, but it is wise action that grows conditions and environments for the greater good. It is only in the doing, through the learning, application and reflection, that organizations will see the 4Cs, not as some fad or fetish, but as fundamental to an organization developing and realizing its potential.

Getting started: preparing the ground

In preparing the ground for 4C transformation your will organization engage with:

1 Coherence makers

   How will coherence makers support 4C transformation?

2 The big questions

   Have all the pre-condition questions for 4C transformational vision, culture, structure, strategies and integration, collaborative partnerships, learning and evaluation been addressed?

3 Transformative learning

   How will learning and transforming mindsets underpin transformation?

4 Paradoxical wisdom

   Why and how are paradoxes and wisdom integral to 4C transformation?

Now the ground is prepared, the next chapter explores how organizations make transformation happen.

4

Making transformation happen

How many pessimists does it take to change a light bulb?

None, it's a waste of time because the new bulb probably won't even work anyway.

FIGURE 4.1 *Light bulb jokes shed light on human anxieties.*

Perhaps the reason there are so many light bulb jokes is because change is ever present and yet difficult to manage and define. In our contemporary world, it seems like transformation is a constant. Yet there are still many examples where transformation has gone badly wrong creating huge damage to the reputation of organizations or to the people within them, ultimately imperiling the survival of those organizations. This chapter deals with how transformation can be considered not as a 'one off' but as a constant feature of organizations. We argue transformation can be a constant if it is understood and practised through the 4Cs: creativity, critical reflection, communication and collaboration.

This chapter explores how to make transformation happen, it examines the big picture considerations of organizational change, and then explores how human potential and organizational effectiveness are harnessed for transformation. We use two coherence makers to support the complex process of learning and developing human capacities for 4C transformation.

The first coherence maker is the Organizational Effectiveness Wheel that enables understanding and to focus on the individual capacities required to build a successful and productive organization. The second coherence maker is the Deep Learning Diamond that explains the nature of the experiences needed for the development and delivery of these capacities. Through case studies of transformation we consider the lessons for effective transformation and provide some reflections on how organizations can become agile and wise as they learn through and in response to change.

So, what is the 'big picture' nature of transformation and how should organizations consider and approach it? Unless your organization is a start-up working in a greenfield site without any legacy, transformation is going to be part of your on-going organizational language, practice, history and future. While we often dream of working from 'scratch' the reality is that we all work within systems, organizations, cultures and structures that require rethinking and shifting as we face emerging internal and external challenges. To begin this exploration of the 'how' of change we are going to take the opportunity to look at a case study of transformation.

Transform or perish – how Save The Children International saved itself

Save the Children International (SCI) is a non-government organization (NGO) that has undergone a complex and sustained transformation in the last few decades. It is one of the largest and oldest aid and development agencies in the world. In 2016, its turnover was US$2.1[1] billion and in that year its programmes reached fifty-six million children.[2] As an organization it has significant influence over policy change through its work in sixty countries.[3] In 1990, the organization looked very different. At that time, SCI was not a consolidated and coherent organization; rather it was a set of individualized and country specific organizations that had little or no unity. This led to their share of total funding slipping, compared to other comparable aid agencies. Additionally disputes between Save the Children country organizations consumed much of their time and took away from their primary goal – supporting children in need internationally.

By 2010 the organization had gone through a massive change process that saw all of the individual organizations collaborate to create an international alliance. The 14,000 employees from country organizations combined into a unified line-management structure.[4] This change was required to transform an organization established in the realities of 1919 to the super competitive and globalized realities of the twenty-first century. Individual and country-based donors now expected a level of consistency in terms of the organization's governance, structure and purpose. SCI was in an environment of increased competition for donations, an expectation of modernized management structures and transparent organizational arrangements. The old structure that featured twenty-nine individual country-based organizations could not deliver consistency to meet these complex needs, yet they did have some advantages. Local organizations in different countries allowed for decentralization that could access diverse and different local resources (including staff, local knowledge etc.) to deliver for the organization. The alliance plan (also known as the 2020 plan) created a 'hub and spoke' organizational arrangement where an international unified governance structure was developed to support the spokes situated in each member country (twenty-nine in all).

At the heart of this transformation was SCI's core purpose to maximize the organization's effectiveness to benefit children. Charlotte Petri Gornitzka, a member of the SCI alliance board remembers it this way:

> We didn't start with a decision about what would be the right organizational structure ... instead we focused on thinking about what children need, what the relevant role for Save the Children was, and what we were good at. Structural changes followed our determination of the impact we wanted to have for children.[5]

But no matter how profound or important the organizational purpose, transformation is always difficult. Rudy von Bernuth was Director of International Programs and led much of the transformation process. He argues that the pace of change was critical in that process of transformation: 'If we moved too slowly we risked losing momentum. There were high expectations and we feared the "Obama effect" of not fulfilling our promises. If we moved too fast, however, we risked making huge mistakes that would unravel the change process.'[6]

With the benefit of hindsight, it is obvious that an organization such as SCI needed to change a structure that had remained largely unchanged since 1919. The reality is that this kind of change is always difficult, especially in an organization as complex as SCI. What SCI achieved was a transformation that modernized its processes and approaches, but kept the distinctiveness of all its individual in-country operations, to deliver more effectively for the children who were ultimately its key stakeholders. SCI argue that this transformation has led to more powerful advocacy for its causes in the media and to government[7] and has simplified its management processes. Jasmine Whitbread, CEO of SCI in 2010 argued:

> We asked ourselves, "What are the fundamental tenets of a twenty-first-century organization with a mission like ours?" First and foremost, it is about being a catalyst. It is not just about delivering great programs on the ground, which is our stock-in-trade and what we know how to do. Second, it is also about being able to communicate what we are doing, to learn from what we are doing—inside the organization but, critically, with other players as well. We are not the only people working on these issues. We are trying to use knowledge to help to create change.[8]

In their view this ensures greater efficiencies and effectiveness. Of course, these changes have not solved all of the organization's problems – no transformation ever can. In some ways, the rapidly shifting world around us reminds organizations of the need to make transformation constant rather than a one off event.

Analysing transformation – aspects of change

One of the key benefits of case studies of transformation is our ability to use hindsight as an analytical tool to understand the 'how' of change. In the following section of this chapter we will consider some of the key aspects of the SCI case study to understand some specific aspects of this process, including:

1 purpose,

2 communication,

3 pace of change,

4   building a culture for transformation,

5   transformation for organizational agility.

Purpose

There is nothing more dispiriting than change for change's sake. The purpose in SCI's case was relatively specific – to create a clear and coherent governance structure to deliver for children in need. As organizations consider the need for transformation the purpose needs to be clear, coherent and related directly to the overall mission of the organization. Organizational transformation academics Ward and Uhl analysed thirteen case studies of organizations undergoing change and argue that transformation 'must have a clear strategic rationale explained in a language which everyone can understand. Otherwise there will be little motivation to change.'[9] The need for explicit and clear purposes that articulate with the internal and external forces on organizations need to be clearly stated in the case for change. Elsbeth Johnson[10] argues in the *Harvard Business Review* that there are four aspects of purpose (or strategic rationale) that organizations must make explicit

1   Why do we need to change, and why now?

2   What is the full extent of the change we need?

3   If we figure out 1 and 2, what should improve as a result? How will we measure the improvement we have been targeting?

4   How does this new strategy or change link to previous strategies?

In SCI's case these questions were addressed but they required integration with a clear communication strategy. The communication strategy needed to make sense to their stakeholders and could simultaneously build trust and momentum for the transformation agenda. Implicit in a clear purpose for an organization is communicating that purpose in accessible language and explaining its implications for stakeholders.

Communication

We talk in depth about communication in Chapter 7 but it is worth taking time here to acknowledge the centrality of communication in the transformation process. Anyone who has been through a 'restructure', a 'harmonization' or a 're-organization' knows that rumour and gossip will fill a gap that is left when communication is vague, lacks purpose or is non-existent. Jasmine Whitbread, CEO of SCI, argues that communication actually builds trust in transforming organizations:

> There's a lot of talk about the need for communication in a change or transformation. I think we have all gotten that message now. We all know how to make sure that we have good two-way communication. But there is a difference between communication and building trust and understanding. Do not underestimate the need to continue to have that trust and understanding with a small group of people, and then continue to foster it. Do not take it for granted, and build out from that a wider and wider constituency for change.[11]

In SCI's case the communication was not just 'nice to have' it was deeply embedded in the confidence of those creating the transformation. In this case and many like it, communication allows organizations to build confidence and trust as the difficult transformation process moves from stage to stage.

The pace of change

There is no 'right' pace for change. What might be right for a large non-government organization may not be right for a small or medium-sized enterprise. In SCI's case the original target for transformation by 2020, identified in the 1990s, moved faster than originally anticipated in response to the demands of stakeholders. The SCI's development of a 'coalition of the willing' and their ability to bring the organization along with them, allowed the transformation timeframe to be achieved more expeditiously (more than ten years earlier than expected). The pace of change is dictated by the ability of an organization to develop a purposeful, effectively communicated and agile transformation.

Of course, the ramifications of transformation that moves too fast or too slow are familiar to many who have suffered through these kinds of change. Rushed transformation is typically led by a leadership group with little connection to the realities of the change. This kind of change leaves the organization vulnerable to internal and external losses of confidence and typically results in high quality employees leaving to find 'better options'. Transformation that is too slow also frustrates. In this scenario organizations seem to be endlessly transforming without much progress and leading to uncompetitiveness, irrelevance and a lack of dynamism. This prolonged process often corrodes the confidence of external stakeholders and leaves the organization vulnerable to ever accelerating external change in demand, competition, technology and regulations.

Building a culture for transformation

Culture is crucial to the transformation process but it also provides an aim. What is the culture that your organization aspires to? In our work with organizations we often connect first with the 'willing and able' to support transformation (in the same way Lego and SCI did). This approach reflects the reality that organizations can spend an enormous amount of time dealing with resistance and not change anything substantive. Our approach, rather, is to seek out those at all levels of an organization who want to be part of the change, are convinced of the need to change and have the capacity to support change rather than spend inordinate amounts of time, energy and resources on those who are not convinced. This group is not a bunch of 'yes people'. They are often questioning and critically reflective, but convinced of the need for transformation.

That is not to say that those who are not convinced are not worthy of being part of the process, it may be a case for some of 'not yet'. Often we find as transformation occurs, people become more persuaded by the opportunities and feel that they can connect more effectively with the approach. Jasmine Whitbread, CEO of SCI during their transformation relied on a similar cultural approach. She counsels:

> Make sure you have laid your groundwork. Make sure that you do have a core group—and it need not be that large—of key players who are totally up for going on that journey with you. Really nurture and do not underestimate the value of that group. Bit by bit, try to broaden that group.[12]

In essence, her approach at SCI was to build a small and committed team, and then as trust and confidence spread, broaden the team responsible for the transformation. Some might argue this is merely strategy, in our view it builds a proactive, positive culture for transformation that expands as others gain confidence in the process. While this is a strategy for transformation it is also a strategy to build an organizational culture that can foster agility in the face of changing circumstances.

Transformation for organizational agility

As we mentioned earlier, organizations can no longer sit still – transformation has become a constant. One of the features of organizations which understand this reality is that they build transformation practices or ongoing agile practice within their organizations. For us, agility is the ability for organizations to learn in response to external and internal factors and act wisely to reshape their practices, policies and approaches while remaining secure and stable. While this kind of organizational flexibility might seem desirable in and of itself, according to a 2017 study by consultancy firm McKinsey,[13] agility also enhances efficiency and effectiveness:

Eighty-one percent of respondents in agile units report a moderate or significant increase in overall performance since their transformations began. And on average, respondents in agile units are 1.5 times more likely than others to report financial outperformance relative to peers, and 1.7 times more likely to report outperforming their peers on nonfinancial measures.

As we explore the role of the 4Cs in the next few chapters of this book we hope you will see how a learning organization can apply these capacities wisely to make their organizations not only transformed but sustained through agility.

The case of Save the Children International underscores the gravity of getting the 'how' of transformation right. If this organization had not managed to transform itself, it was not shareholders or customers who lost out, it was the most vulnerable children in our community who would have suffered. In this sense, and in so many others, the 'how' of transformation is not an 'academic' pursuit, it is the difference between the survival and demise of an organization that often has profound ramifications for many in our community.

What is the 'stuff' of transformation?

The Save the Children case study reveals the big picture of successful transformation in an organization. It is an overarching view that deals with the components of our 4C leadership framework discussed in the previous chapter and it involves the re-imagining and re-shaping of Save the Children's vision, culture, structure and strategy. What then underpins the overarching frame of transformation, what exactly makes change from within? What energies, thinking and human capacities actually support the big picture of transformation? This is where we argue that certain capacities can be developed and strengthened in the way work and learning happens in an organization. For an organization to be agile and transforming, individuals within it have to be agile and transforming.

Communicating a vision, changing structures and implementing strategies are enablers of change but it is not the 'stuff' that inhabits the change. The stuff of change is human potential. How that potential is realized becomes a learning challenge for organizations. How do people best learn how to unlearn old ways and learn new ways? How do they develop agility and the 4Cs? In our work with organizations, we begin with a coherence maker that focuses organizations on the human capacities required for transformation; it is the Organizational Effectiveness Wheel (OEW).

Coherence makers such as the OEW bring clarity to understanding something quite complex like building human potential and developing organizational effectiveness. As discussed in Chapter 3, coherence makers should never be understood or used as something simplistic or reductive. Coherence makers are fundamental understandings that open up and out to greater complexity and connections in phenomenon and experiences. Coherence makers are a construct to make the complex tangible, knowable and learnable. At the same time coherence makers should allow for continued exploration and discovery of a phenomenon or experience. In this case the OEW summarizes, identifies and articulates the human capacities that make an organization capable of transforming.

The Organizational Effectiveness Wheel (OEW)

The Organizational Effectiveness Wheel (Figure 4.2) is a coherence maker that describes the capacities that can be found in a dynamic and effective organization. It can describe the individual in an organization, and it can describe the organization as a corporate entity. The OEW is also used as a diagnostic tool to analyse and evaluate the strengths and weaknesses of an organization's

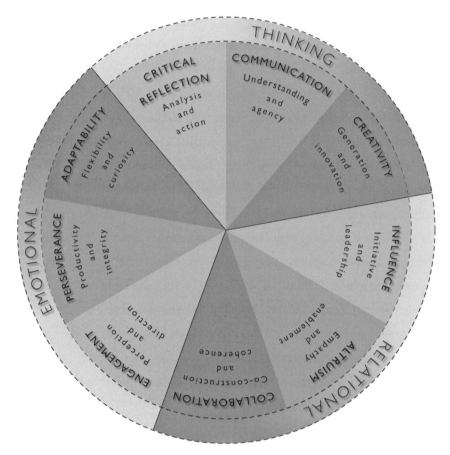

FIGURE 4.2 *The Organizational Effectiveness Wheel (OEW) focuses organizations on the capacities required for 4C transformation.*

thinking, relational and emotional climate for transformation. This gives leadership an opportunity to develop the 10,000 km high birds-eye view of the organization, a viewpoint that develops an organization's effectiveness in *critical reflection*. To build the organization's capacities in all areas of the OEW, overall strengths of the organization are recognized to address weaknesses. Through surveys, questioning and discussions, certain capacities of the OEW emerge as starting points for development, enhancement and refinement.

The OEW is used as a macro-lens to give a panoramic overview of the organization, and it can also be used as a microscopic lens to recognize and develop individual capacities. In an organization we worked with recently, a number of individuals were appointed to newly created leadership roles to build greater staff responsibility and agency. Using the OEW as a diagnostic tool it became apparent these individuals needed development in the social skills of *collaboration* and *influence*. To develop their leadership skills would empower them as people of influence and strengthen the organization's climate and culture for change. As a diagnostic, the OEW highlights starting points from which to build the human potential for organizational transformation. The OEW continues to assess the on-going effectiveness of the capacities of the organization and of the individuals, and diagnoses what to develop and strengthen next. We argue an organization as an entity, and the individuals within the organization, can develop all the attributes of the Organizational Effectiveness Wheel through the 4C processes explored in this book.

The OEW is based on the US National Research Council's report, *Education for Life and Work: Developing Transferable Knowledge and Skills in the 21st Century*,[14] and draws from research in developmental, educational, organizational and social psychology, and economics. The OEW describes how skills in thinking (cognition), the relational (the interpersonal) and emotional regulation (the intrapersonal) are essential for building human potential and organizational effectiveness.[15] The capacities in the OEW are integral and co-dependent. What this means is, you cannot develop one capacity such as *creativity* without all the other aspects of the OEW. Table 4.1 describes the interdependent capacities on the OEW. A transforming organization has to consider these capacities in the organizational climate and culture, and in individual capacities. As we work with organizations we have found the efficacy of the OEW is revealed when using it as a diagnostic tool, but it also has other benefits as a coherence maker for transformation.

TABLE 4.1 *Capacities in the Organizational Effectiveness Wheel*

Thinking

The cognitive involves capacities for thinking, reasoning, interpreting and generating ideas.

Critical reflection
    Analysis and action

Complex problem solving through analysis, evaluation and action.

Communication
    Understanding and agency

Understanding and expressing meaning through agency.

Creativity
    Generation and innovation

Generating and innovating inventive ideas and enterprises.

Emotional

The intrapersonal involves capacities for managing behaviours and emotions to achieve a goal.

Adaptability
    Flexibility and curiosity

Continually learning by being flexible and curious about changing perspectives and circumstances.

Perseverance
    Productivity and integrity

Showing determination and integrity to achieve a productive outcome.

Engagement
    Perception and direction

Making perceptive choices and focusing on a positive direction.

Relational

The interpersonal involves capacities for expressing, interpreting and relating to others.

Influence
    Initiative and leadership

Taking initiative and responsibility to lead others through influence and guidance.

Altruism
    Empathy and enablement

Using empathy and compassion to enable all to thrive and benefit from decisions and actions.

Collaboration
    Co-construction and coherence

Connecting with others to generate and co-construct ideas and actions in a collective endeavour.

The OEW as a coherence maker

In organizations, coherence makers can develop:

- a common language,
- metacognition (*engagement*), and
- positive belief in learning.

A common language

Coherence makers provide organizations with a common language to talk about processes such as the 4Cs or OEW capacities. A common language about capacities and processes leads to common understanding and shared meaning. In our work we hear leadership and staff in organizations use the language of coherence makers to develop strategies and processes to address issues and ideas. For instance, they refer to *offering and yielding* (from the Collaboration Circles coherence maker in chapter 8) when developing collaboration skills, or *identifying assumptions* when re-solving a problem (from the Critical Reflection Crucible in chapter 6), or *playing with possibility* when trying to generate a new idea (from the Creativity Cascade in chapter 5), or they consider how to develop staff *engagement* or *altruism* in work practices, or *perseverance* in certain tasks (from the OEW capacities, Figure 4.2).

A common language or metalanguage helps organizations to focus on and explore processes and capacities through a shared understanding of what they are. It is not simply about using jargon, it has to be language that is understood and used through active experience. *Offering and yielding* as a process is a term that only makes sense when it is physically experienced and practised. Language gives a name to a shared process, and it also builds metacognition of the process.

Metacognition

The OEW as a coherence maker is useful in bringing both clarity and complexity to understanding the component parts of an organization's effectiveness and an individual's potential. Bringing attention, awareness and thinking (*engagement*) to capacities in the OEW develops metacognition. Metacognition is the ability to be aware of, understand and control your own cognition or thinking so that through forethought and self-reflection, adjustments to behaviours and actions can be made. Through metacognition the ability to learn, unlearn and relearn is strengthened:

> Metacognition refers to a person's ability to select, monitor, manage, and evaluate cognitive processing during the learning or performance of a cognitive task. Metacognition strategies are higher-level methods for managing one's thinking and reasoning while learning or performing a task. Metacognitive strategies may play a central role in people's ability to transfer – that is, in people's ability to solve new problems and learn new things.[16]

Metacognition is central to learning capacities and developing a positive belief that learning is possible.

Positive belief in learning

All capacities on the OEW can be developed, for an organization's climate and culture can change,[17] and an individual's capacity can develop.[18] The OEW as a coherence maker does two things, it describes the overall capacities for an effective organization and it describes the specific competencies that individuals need. It is a self-reinforcing cycle of building organizational capacity with individual competencies. An organization's ability and an individual's ability to learn, develop and employ *creativity, critical reflection, communication, collaboration, influence, altruism, engagement, perseverance* and *adaptability* is not fixed or set in stone. These are capacities that in the right environment and conditions can be inculcated, learnt and continually developed. Therefore an organizational climate and individual capacities are malleable and can develop and change.

Changes in individual capacity and personality are as much determined by the environment as by genes.[19] The environment then is as much determined by individual personalities as by the beliefs and assumptions of culture. This means if you are in a *creative, critically reflective, communicative* and *collaborative* environment you will become more *creative, critically reflective, communicative* and *collaborative*. If there are conditions that support the individual development of *engagement, perseverance, adaptability, influence* and *altruism*, the more these capacities become the DNA and culture of an organization.

Human brain architecture can be developed and re-wired through neuroplasticity and the conditions and environment of an organization (see Chapter 3). Knowing that the capacity to learn and change is not fixed but possible, creates a positive belief or 'growth mindset'. A growth mindset affects how you approach developing capacities, as psychology professor Carol Dweck explains:

> In this mindset, the hand you're dealt is just the starting point for development. This growth mindset is based on the belief that your basic qualities are things you can cultivate through your efforts. Although people may differ in every which way – their initial talents and aptitudes, interests or temperaments – everyone can change and grow through application and experience.[20]

Positive and productive beliefs are key to developing the emotional aspects (*engagement, perseverance* and *adaptability*) in the OEW, which are then integral to building the other thinking and relational capacities.[21] Capacity is a dynamic between innate ability and the disposition we develop towards learning. As a coherence maker the OEW demonstrates that learning skills and processes in the capacities are possible, which then encourages a positive belief necessary to develop them. A common language, metacognition and a positive belief in learning are needed to develop the 4Cs, but they alone are not enough.

For 4C processes and capacities to be learnt, developed and inculcated requires experiences that are described as deeper learning. The 4Cs of creativity, critical reflection, communication and collaboration can only be learnt and understood when applied authentically in an organizational context; they cannot be a one-off or occasional project. As discussed in Chapter 3, the 4Cs are a mindset and culture that only exist as processes in action, authentically applied to the work of an organization. Crucially, learning and developing the 4Cs must be an on-going and authentic process towards transformation. To understand and highlight deeper learning in 4C processes and transformation, we will use a case study that involves a number of public service organizations dealing with highly complex and seemingly insurmountable issues: the Glasgow Effect.

Case study: the Glasgow Effect

Glasgow in western Scotland was once revered as a leading centre of shipbuilding, steel-making and engineering but in 2008 Glasgow became known for having some of the worst health outcomes and life expectancy gaps

FIGURE 4.3 *Children playing in the Gorbals tenement courtyard in Glasgow, Scotland in 1970.*

in Europe. The World Health Organization[22] reported that a boy living in a deprived district of Glasgow had an average life expectancy of fifty-four years compared to a boy from an affluent area seven miles away, who could expect to live to eighty-two. The stark health inequalities came to be known as the Glasgow Effect. The conventional wisdom was Glaswegians had a poor diet (fried Mars bars and fried haggis), heightened tobacco and alcohol consumption that led to heart disease and especially cancer. Deeper inquiries into the issue questioned these assumptions and found the story was far more complex.

The gap in life expectancy between the rich and poor in Glasgow had always existed, but in the 1960s it began to widen even more. Sir Harry Burns, former Chief Medical Officer for Scotland explains what happened at the time:

> You could see disintegration of communities as post-war housing booms started to take over, the old tenement buildings in Glasgow were being knocked down, and they should have been knocked down because they were no longer fit for human habitation, there were outside toilets and so on. But what replaced them did not facilitate community connectedness.[23]

People had been living in poverty in the tenement areas but they had supported each other in their circumstances. In the 1960s they were moved to council estates on the periphery of Glasgow, and at the same time the shipyards and car factories were closing down and people were losing their jobs.

The new hypothesis for the poor health and life expectancy of the Glasgow Effect was that social fragmentation and instability had caused a long-lasting and dire effect on poor populations in Glasgow. The life expectancy gap when looked at closely ten years before revealed there was a cohort effect impacting trends, not older people dying earlier. The main causes were drugs, alcohol, violence, mental health problems and suicide in younger people from thirty to thirty-five. Ten years later the effect is evident in the same cohort at forty to forty-five years old. The cohort effect suggests that 'something happened to them that predisposed them to socially determined ill-health that led them to die of drugs and alcohol and suicide and so on'.[24] Epigenetic influences also emerged as a factor, where the stressful environment in childhood was switching on certain genes. The conventional medical approach to deal with these problems would be prevention programmes for smoking and drug use, and drugs for heart disease and mental health. Instead, social and biological factors causing instability and stress, disconnection and disempowerment, needed to be addressed.

According to Harry Burns, now Professor of Global Health at the University of Strathclyde in Glasgow, 'To crack difficult lives, we need to discover what is really wrong in those lives and seek to transform them.'[25] Rather than focus on deficits in the health inequities, Burns argues the focus should be on building human assets and social capital so that individuals can offer each other friendship and mutual support. But to build social capital needed a new organizational approach in public health and public service interventions to deal with an issue like the Glasgow Effect.

The conventional way of doing health policy is public servants and some experts devising an intervention and then passing it on to front line staff to implement. Many organizations across government and private sectors implement and deliver in this way, but in Harry Burns' view it does not work. He argues that, when 'frontline staff haven't been involved in shaping the intervention, they're not particularly enthusiastic about it and often it's not implemented appropriately'.[26]

Instead, a new approach called the Early Years Collaborative was developed that was a radical departure in the way intervention and delivery was designed. The aim of the approach was 'to get frontline staff to design the intervention, because they see the people who need help'.[27] Not only were the interventions based on the first-hand experiences of frontliners in the community, the interventions also worked across public service sectors and systems. Burns explains,

Over the past five years we've asked staff involved in supporting parents and children to come up with ideas, test them, and if they see an improvement, spread that learning across the collaborative. So people were being brought together regularly to discuss what had worked and what hadn't worked, and then try to implement things consistently.[28]

The Early Years Collaborative approach aims to address the issue of the Glasgow Effect from multiple perspectives, experiences and expertise. Rather than working from a head office, the Early Years Collaborative works on the frontline across the silos of family and community services, the health system and education, and across public, private and voluntary sectors. All the services collaborate on what they want to achieve, and agree on the methods, measurement, feedback and evidence they will use. As a result there has been a significant decrease in stillbirth rates and infant mortality, a decrease in deaths of children in hospital, an improved uptake of services such as child assessments, improved support and monitoring in child development, improved readiness and performance for learning at school and so on. The approach is being further developed for young people as they go through other significant transitions such as primary to secondary school, and leaving school to employment. For public sector organizations, it is a very different way of doing things, it does not involve 'doing things "to" people, it's supporting young people to do things for themselves.'[29]

An example of one of the many initiatives is the GalGael Trust, a charity that is a focal point for craft courses and community activity in Glasgow. According to the founding director, Alistair McIntosh,[30] their courses teach more than crafts:

A project like this calls back the soul into a community. It brings back even the most broken people their sense of self-worth . . . it helps people reconnect with their cultural roots, express creativity they never knew they had and develop networks and life skills to counter addictions and other health problems.

The outcomes of an approach such as the Early Years Collaborative are over a time scale of ten to fifteen years, well beyond the short-term agendas of the usual policy and political cycles. As an intervention, the Early Years Collaborative is transforming public service delivery and policy.

Analysing transformation

Transforming people's lives is the focus of the Early Years Collaborative. It is an approach that focuses on promoting health and wellbeing, rather than those that cause disease. The Early Years Collaborative is also a 4C transformation of the public service's organizational structure, culture and approach. The 4Cs are apparent in the case study in these ways: The Early Years Collaborative applied *critical reflection* processes to the issue (the Glasgow Effect), and assumptions were identified and contested, and new hypotheses developed to continue re-solving the issue. *Creativity* was evident in the possibilities developed by staff from their frontline observations to address the issue from a multitude of perspectives. *Collaboration* across sectors in the Early Years Collaborative was key to unifying and magnifying the effectiveness of the interventions and their delivery. *Communication* was enabling the voice of frontline staff and the community they were working with to generate productive and positive action. In the Early Years Collaborative approach there is also evidence of 'deeper learning'.

4C processes and OEW (Figure 4.2) capacities including:

- adaptability
- perseverance
- engagement
- collaboration
- critical reflection
- communication
- creativity
- influence
- altruism

must involve experiences of deeper learning to be transformative. We introduce another coherence maker, the Deep Learning Diamond (see Figure 4.4) to

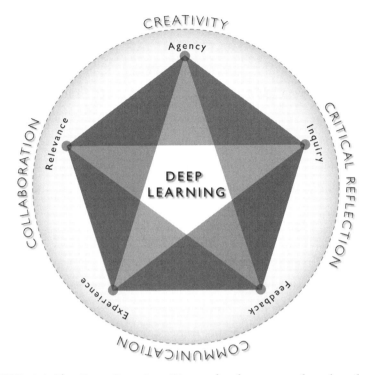

FIGURE 4.4 *The Deep Learning Diamond coherence maker describes the components of deeper learning.*

explain the complex components of deeper learning experiences. The Deep Learning Diamond identifies the components *agency, inquiry, feedback, experiences* and *relevance* as key to developing transformative learning experiences. In the Deep Learning Diamond diagram the ring of the 4Cs surround the components of *agency, inquiry, feedback, experiences* and *relevance*, and within the 4Cs all these components are related and affect each other. *Agency, inquiry, feedback, experiences* and *relevance* that support deeper learning are evident in the Glasgow case study. We explain what these components mean, and how they are exhibited in the story of the Early Years Collaborative.

Agency: empowerment and self-direction

Agency is the power to take action, and it comes from a sense of empowerment derived from confidence, opportunity and capacity. Agency strengthens autonomy, self-belief and self-worth. In the Early Years Collaborative, agency was given to frontline workers when they were given 'ownership' of their interventions. Staff at the frontline knew the people they were helping and knew how to develop and shape the interventions they were implementing. By having agency, staff members were precise, committed and enthusiastic in what they were doing. With greater autonomy they were more self-regulated and self-directed in their work. Learning is deepened when actions are more mindfully and effectively undertaken through the empowerment of self-direction.

Agency is also apparent in the encounters and processes the frontline staff have with the community. The Early Years Collaborative (and the Raising Attainment Collaborative) recognizes that engagement with young people needs not to be doing things 'to' them, but supporting them to act for themselves. Working with parents from backgrounds of poverty, domestic violence and parental mental health issues, is also a process of reaching out to empower and help them support the children. The confidence and self-worth that comes with agency has to be built as a capacity, and developed as an opportunity through creative, critical reflective, communicative and collaborative processes. Agency to think and act for yourself is strengthened through inquiry.

Inquiry: valuing questions over answers

Tackling the Glasgow Effect and understanding poor health outcomes can only be explored and deepened as a learning inquiry. Inquiry is to approach everything with questions, rather than answers that are quick fix, knee jerk, one-size fits all and procedurally compliant. The reality is that re-solving problems and generating new ideas is complex and requires a deeper, multi-layered, many perspectives approach. Depth, layers and perspectives can only be analysed through the quality questions of inquiry. By asking the frontline staff to design the Early Years Collaborative interventions, they used inquiry to generate ideas and then tested them to see improvements. Inquiry then was integral to health delivery, rather than a superficial and procedural approach.

An inquiry approach is to always ask 'why, really why?' something is a phenomenon or experience. It never takes anything as a given, for assumptions underpin everything we do and observe.[31] Inquiry requires awareness and very strong powers of observation, but inquiry itself begins to develop perceptions and insights. Inquiry as an on-going critical and reflective mindset is essential to a deeper understanding of anything, including the 4Cs. Inquiry is refined through on-going feedback.

Feedback: iteration with experimentation

Any inquiry can only be developed through timely feedback, so testing and analysing results and outcomes among the Early Years Collaborative was critical to learning from their interventions. The feedback informed their work, and through regular discussions their work was constantly refined and re-assessed for more effective and consistent implementation. In the big data assessments, it was sometimes difficult to ascertain which Early Years Collaborative interventions had produced what change, and this is due to a multi-pronged inquiry approach dealing with great complexity. The overall positive outcomes, however, supported the continuing of the Early Years Collaborative approach, but feedback as evidence is critical for policy makers and bureaucrats in organizations in terms of funding decisions. The spectacular improvements achieved by the Early Years Collaborative convinced bureaucrats to fund the new approach.

Feedback is an on-going, iterative and collaborative process that builds strengths and addresses weaknesses to find possible forward directions. Feedback as reflection and evaluation is fundamental to an organization's growth through the 4Cs, but this can only be achieved through the impact of emotional, relational and cognitive experiences and conditions.

Experiences: emotional, relational, thinking capacities

Reflecting on valuable experiences at the frontline developed the approach and interventions by the Early Years Collaborative. Learning experiences have to be conducive to growth,[32] so the interaction between the frontline staff and the community has to be positive emotionally and relationally, to support an effective intervention. One of the interventions, Bedtime Bear, involved children being given a teddy bear that needed a bedtime story every night. Bedtime Bear encouraged children to ask parents to give them the positive experience of a bedtime story. This intervention is an experience that consciously develops emotional and relational aspects with the cognitive intervention, that is not only between parent and child, but also between the frontline staff and the community.

Experiences that are transformative are learning experiences that are social, psychological and physically embodied.[33] The ability to think and reason is linked to how we control our emotions and how we relate to others, and these factors are genetic and shaped by the context around us.[34] Our social environment impacts our development as individuals, and learning is an interaction of our disposition with our social experiences.[35] The processes of creativity, critical reflection, communication and collaboration must be inhabited as social, embodied and reflective experiences to affect an individual's and an organization's growth and development. The experiences must also be relevant to have impact.

Relevance: in-context application

The Early Years Collaborative demonstrates how the 4Cs are only really understood as embodied experiences authentically applied to a context. The 4Cs have to be applied to a real context otherwise they are abstract concepts that are mission statements, good ideas in theory, and nothing more. A head office disconnected from the community was not concocting policy; the interventions were based on frontline staff's authentic and relevant experiences with the community. By being on the ground, and being across sectors, the

Early Years Collaborative interventions were relevant by realizing how complex, multi-faceted and connected the issues are.

4C processes are on-going learning

Developing 4C processes with *agency, inquiry, feedback, experiences* and *relevance* establishes confidence and belief in the human capacity for transformation, and communities and organizations to thrive.[36] The capacities of the OEW and 4C processes do, however, require new learning, un-learning and re-learning through application, practise and reflection. For instance, it is by experiencing obstacles and setbacks, and achieving results from productivity and integrity that *perseverance*, determination and resilience are developed. Developing capacities and processes through application, practise and reflection is educationally sound and logical, but in our experience, most organizations treat learning (including those in educational institutions) as a one off experience, that ticks a box, and may or may not necessarily be embedded into re-imagined practices. Crucially, the application of 4C processes must be authentic to real work situations and issues, and when it succeeds or fails in practice it must be reflected upon and developed with others collaboratively in the workplace.

To implement the 4Cs in an organization requires a 4C process: it must be collaborative and critically reflective, communicative and creative. Organizations, however, can be frenetic, busy places and there are challenges in prioritizing time and effort for a 4C approach. We argue that putting time and energy into these processes is wise as a long-term investment. The payoff is an agile and adaptive organization that at its heart has a 4C culture based in on-going learning and transformation. In Glasgow's case this has translated into public service and private sector organizations in partnership, delivering more successful health and social outcomes focusing on wellness rather than illness, and in doing so transforming the lives of a community.

4Cs for transformation and wisdom

Each 'C' is a process for learning that when deeply understood and practised continually opens up reflection, possibility, action, challenge and connections. These dynamics are evident in the coherence makers we present in the 'C' chapters (Chapters 4–8) – the creativity cascade, critical reflection crucible, communication crystal, and collaboration circles. Learning through the 4C processes has to be generative, that is, it has to perpetuate and sustain on-going learning. Deeper or generative learning is to build learning onto what we already know, and we argue the 4Cs are the motor for deeper, on-going and agile learning that powers on-going reflection and re-invention of the work of the organization.

What is also vital to the success of an organization is a culture that values the learning of wisdom. Without wisdom, organizations act without foresight and insight in the sustainability of the organization, as well as the greater good. Learning in wisdom is recognized as a much-needed dimension in the leadership and social fabric of organizations. Wisdom is imperative in business, leadership and management and organizational learning, for without wisdom, organizations are in the hands of self-interest and expedience, imprudence, short-termism, waste, injustice, avarice and abuse. Clever, new ideas without wisdom are Enron's high-risk accounting practices, or Lehman Brothers' leveraging in subprime mortgages, or Volkswagen's de-activation of emissions control systems, or Cambridge Analytica's exploitation of data through Facebook. Wisdom guides ethical behaviour, and makes sound and reasoned judgements in decision-making and actions. In our view practical wisdom is integral to 4C processes, and the 4Cs are a way of re-integrating wisdom conceptually and practically into the working life of an organization.

Making transformation happen is to take the optimist's view that change is possible. Possibility is harnessed when the purpose, communication and pace of change of transformation are clarified and communicated. Possibility is to build an organizational culture that fosters agility and learning by developing human potential and capacities in the Organizational Effectiveness Wheel. These capacities are deepened when there is self-directed agency; learning as inquiry and feedback; and emotional, relational and cognitive experiences that are relevant and applied in the context of an organization's work (the Deep Learning Diamond). With knowledge in 4C processes and skills, optimists can make transformation happen.

How many optimists does it take change a light bulb?

None, they're convinced the power will come back on soon.

Getting started: making transformation happen

Making transformation happen requires an organization to ask the following questions.

For 4C transformation how is the organization considering, exploring and developing:

1 Communication

How will the purpose and pace of change be communicated to the organization?

2 A culture of learning

How will the 4Cs create an agile learning culture where transformation is a constant?

3 Human potential

How will the Organizational Effectiveness Wheel be used as a coherence maker and diagnostic tool?

4   Deeper learning

How will agency, inquiry, feedback, experiences and relevance be developed in 4C processes?

5   Wisdom

How can wisdom underpin learning in the 4Cs?

The next four chapters explore each of the 4Cs: creativity, critical reflection, communication and collaboration, and explain how their processes work to transform organizations.

5

Creativity

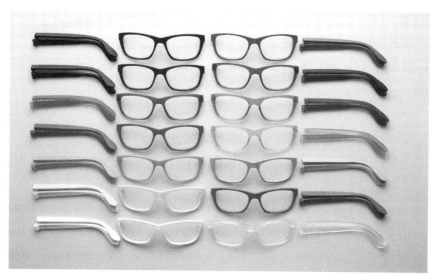

FIGURE 5.1 *Dresden Optic's modular design.*

In our experience working with organizations, creativity is much discussed and little understood. On the one hand, it seems to be the silver bullet that will solve everybody's problems. On the other hand, we encounter people in organizations who claim 'I am not creative', as if creativity were gifted to only a few by some mystical or magical process. In our view, both of these attitudes are not only wrong but they also restrict the opportunity for organizations to meet their full potential. As we discuss in this chapter, creativity is not mystical. It is an inherent human characteristic like communication, so, we introduce a coherence maker for creativity – the Creativity Cascade. We demonstrate the creativity cascade working in practice through a case study of a start-up, Dresden Optics, who made creativity central to their organizations processes and products.

Glasses are to many of us a bit of a necessary nuisance. Perhaps you have never thought of spectacles (including their manufacture, marketing etc.) as particularly creative. Yet there is scope as we explain in this chapter for creativity to be a standard expectation in every industry, sector and throughout organizations. Dresden Optics demonstrates how creativity can emerge in unlikely places and become central to how organizations are constituted, managed and grown.

Dresden Optics

In 2000 Bruce Jeffreys (co-founder of Dresden Optics) went to see a show featuring a DJ in Amsterdam. Nothing particularly unusual there except the show was in an eyewear shop – an optometrist. He wondered after that experience why glasses were such a sterile and seemingly remote experience when they could be much more fun. At that time and since, glasses (worn by around 48 per cent of the population in Europe)[1] were a high-priced necessity. What Bruce Jeffreys noticed was the gap between the actual retail cost of glasses and the actual cost of manufacturing. He noticed a massive mark-up and an industry ripe for disruption. And then he asked himself a number of questions – the *why, really why* questions: Why were glasses so expensive? Why was the customer experience devoid of fun? Why were glasses not more functional and versatile? Why were glasses not more like toothbrushes – cheap, dependable, standardized and easily replaceable?

He formed an optics company and started *playing with possibilities*. Dresden Optics played with different materials for the frames and the lenses. They played with different approaches to branding, retailing and marketing, HR and staffing. For instance, they *played with possibilities* when sourcing materials from the most unlikely places for use in manufacturing the frames. A ranger in the Gulf of Carpentaria in northern Australia who knew of Dresden's approach contacted them with an idea. He had an unlimited supply of abandoned nylon fishing nets (ghost nets) that killed sea life and was an environmental menace. Could these nets be recycled to make the frames for Dresden's glasses? It turned out that they could and now every week a truck full of discarded nets unloads its cargo in a factory in Sydney and recycles the potential landfill into frames for Dresden's glasses.

Dresden's capacity to play with possibilities led to several innovative responses that could now be refined into a business model. The *selecting and evaluating* of the possibilities made them assess all of the approaches they had considered against market realities. What price point would work? What product range and colours would appeal? Would customers be satisfied with only one frame design?

Low-cost glasses, while relatively recent, are not new. Warby Parker in the United States has been making and selling low cost frames since 2010. The point of difference for Dresden, however, is that it has only one frame design (with hundreds of colours – see Figure 5.1). Unlike Warby Parker this allows Dresden to simplify the production process and invest in the customer experience, dramatically reducing the price point and maximizing the margin (Dresden's glasses are less than half the price of Warby Parker's). The result today is a high-technology, environmentally sustainable manufacturing firm with healthy margins and strong export potential. For the customers at Dresden's tens stores in Australia and Canada, it means that they can walk in off the street and have glasses customized for them within ten minutes at a fraction of the price of 'brand name' glasses. The plans for Dresden are ambitious, with aspirations to open between fifty and eighty retail stores and expansion into India, South Africa and New Zealand. They also have plans to provide low-cost eyewear for people who cannot currently afford glasses. Their intent is clear: 'Our mission is to transform people's lives through better vision – enabling them to learn, work and be independent. We're working day and night to bring high-quality, sustainably-made prescription glasses to anyone in the world, no matter where they live and how much money they have.'[2] They have their sights fixed on the over five billion people Dresden claims will need glasses by 2050. This is an ambitious undertaking but the potential benefits of creating a robust yet inexpensive glasses frame, position this small but growing company to respond to this challenge. This could create massive benefits for individuals and communities who are hampered by preventable sight problems.

While this might seem like a fairly straightforward business development process, creativity is apparent throughout this case. Unwittingly perhaps, Bruce Jeffreys and Dresden followed the process of creativity we call the Creativity Cascade. The Creativity Cascade has four components (that we have italicised in the case study): *noticing; asking why?, really why?; playing with possibility*; and *evaluating and selecting*. For Dresden, the business opportunity was made possible through *noticing* that glasses were expensive, and *noticing* the potential to simultaneously make eyewear environmentally sustainable and affordable. The next stage was to ask deep questions, *why?, really why?*, about the business realities of the industry to understand *why, really why* things are as they are and how to change might be possible. In the *playing with possibility* phase, Dresden experimented broadly across all areas of its business. By exploring this process, they found ways to innovate in their systems, manufacturing approaches and approaches to recruiting and HR. Finally, they went through a selection process where they considered the realities of marketing, retail, product development etc. and then *selected and evaluated* an approach to take to market.

Dresden is currently a small player in the international US$102 billion[3] eyewear and optics business but their approach of creativity and constant innovation means that they may not be a small player for long. Dresden's approach does not regard creativity as a remote function of the business but places it at the centre of its processes, approaches and products. This enables this organization and many others like it to re-imagine every aspect of the business to generate benefits for the community, environment and the economy. For Dresden, creativity is not part of the business, it is the way they do business, and is at the centre of the organization. In other words, Dresden have not just thought outside the box – they have re-invented the box.

This call to think 'outside of the box' and make organizations inherently creative and innovative has become a roar lately in business, education and so many other places. The demands of twenty-first century life mean that creativity has moved from being a 'nice to have' to an essential for organizations who want to be agile and responsive to their emerging realities. Consultancy firm Price Waterhouse Coopers (PWC) claims: 'For businesses of all sizes, the challenges brought by technology, complexity and changing customer preferences are driving the need for business model innovation'[4] And if that is not evidence enough, recent research[5] claims that creativity leads to market/sector leadership and 'direct and tangible economic outcomes'.

Mythbusting the 4Cs as aerosol words

In a 2010 study of 1,700 CEOs, 61 per cent[6] of them identified creativity as critical for employees' future success (the survey also identified collaboration (75%), and communication (67%)). The problem is that creativity is an 'aerosol word' that is often sprayed about by managers and leaders because it smells good. The problem is the concept, like aerosol, often vanishes when you try and get hold of it (as we discussed in Chapter 3). While creativity may not be ignored (in many organizations creativity and innovation are frequently discussed) its perceived mystical and unstructured nature (its 'aerosol-ness') makes it difficult to implement. The problem with thinking about creativity as some mysterious and unknowable capacity is that it becomes unattainable, undeliverable and ultimately unrealizable.

For organizations, this kind of vagueness does not support the growth and development of innovation. Nor does it make creativity and innovation a standard expectation of an organizational culture. We believe that creativity is innovation literacy. What we mean by this is that creativity forms the vital building blocks for innovation in the same way that language makes communication possible. If you have no language, communication is almost impossible. The same goes for creativity. If you do not have an understanding of creativity, innovation is almost impossible. And yet organizations often talk about innovation without a working understanding of creativity – its processes and approaches. Creativity researcher Teresa Amabile and her colleagues argue: 'All innovation begins with creative ideas. Successful implementation of new programs, new product introductions, or new services depends on a person or a team having a good idea—and developing that idea beyond its initial state.'[7]

In this chapter, we discuss some of the issues and myths around creativity and provide a process for organizations to make creativity more than a vague concept. The Creativity Cascade that we explore later in this chapter provides a framework for organizations to understand and enact creative processes that lead directly to innovation. In each of the C chapters (Creativity, Critical Reflection, Communication and Collaboration) we will spend some time exploring and exploding myths about the 4Cs. This is to help with the unlearning process. Over the years these terms have been plagued by a lack of clarity and mythology. By discussing the myths, we hope to make them less like aerosol and more like concepts that can be understood and implemented. We will begin by discussing the most mythologised of the Cs, creativity.

Myth 1: Creativity is unknowable

Let's begin with a thought experiment: which is the more tangible, gravity or creativity? If you said gravity you would not be alone. Many people find creativity a difficult concept to grasp, whereas we can always imagine Newton's falling apple when trying to imagine gravity. Perhaps the first image that comes to mind when you think of creativity is people (perhaps astronauts) floating around without any kind of restraint, in outer space or in one of those gravity-free simulators. So, we notice gravity in its absence rather than its presence. We think the same is true of creativity. We often notice the absence of creativity in our workplaces, in our communities and in ourselves rather than its presence. For example, when we work with organizations we often start with the question: 'Who here would call themselves creative?' In almost every organization less than half the group identifies as 'creative' (sometimes fewer than 10 per cent). So, what does a lack of creativity look like in an organization? Typically, in our experience it is a lack of engagement, a lack of excitement and a general lack of dynamism. But it does not need to be this way. Creativity is a definable, knowable and learnable capacity. It is like gravity as a force that has observable features and can be applied to organizations to make them more vital and dynamic. Creativity can also provide a consistent shape for organizations in the same way gravity shapes and organizes our physical world.

To many, creativity is a kind of formless amorphous activity undertaken by genius individuals and without reference to anybody else. This kind of debilitating myth has done damage to the potential for creativity to be useful. We think creativity is as real as gravity and is a solid, heavy concept that is for everyone – not just a gifted few.

Myth 2: Creativity is for a few special individuals and not everyone

Another myth about creativity is that it is an individual process disconnected from others – this is the myth of the heroic artist working individually in an attic (see Figure 5.2). This is sometimes called the 'creative genius' phenomena. While we are not denying that creative geniuses exist, they are the exception rather than the rule and they almost always collaborate with others. Mozart, while obviously a creative genius, could not have been successful without the teachers, mentors and other musicians that contributed to his compositions and performances.

We can see this in the stories organizations tell themselves today. The story usually goes that creativity only exists in certain industries – advertising or marketing – and then only in certain roles. As such, creativity is only for the 'gifted few'. Of course, creativity is an inherency like our need to be in relationship with each other, and like relationships it can be developed and strengthened to deliver better outcomes for organizations.

FIGURE 5.2 *Leonid Pasternak, 'The Passion of Creation' circa 1880.*

This myth is often designed to divide the 'creatives' from the 'non-creatives' or the more widely used euphemism, 'the technicians'. This false dichotomy entrenches the old idea that some are born to creativity and some are born to technicality as if these two cannot interact. Of course, the 'technicians' routinely practice a great deal of creativity. For instance, in making films if those who are called 'creatives' have no understanding of the technical aspects of their work their creativity is likely to be unsuccessful. Creativity is a capacity that often looks different across roles in an organization but is present in every individual and every work role even though it might look different. Creativity is part of our daily lives and exercised by us all. Creativity, like critical reflection, communication or collaboration, is a capacity we can learn, strengthen and develop. We all have the capacity to be creative. Educator and creativity researcher Anna Craft[8] called this, 'lifewide creativity' as it is present and demonstrated every day in our work, sport and social lives, and in many of these contexts creativity is usually collaborative as well.

If you think of examples of organizations that have a reputation for creativity – collaboration is at the heart of what they do. For instance, Apple is one of the most creative organizations in corporate history. The organization has been led by creative individuals, particularly their CEOs and Heads of Design such as Steve Jobs, Johnny Ive, Marc Newsom and more recently Tim Cook, but they did not achieve this as individuals, they collaborated. They all led teams who contributed to the creativity that has been a prime feature of Apple's success. That approach continues with the design of their sprawling campus in Cupertino, Los Angeles which has designed collaboration into the building with large, open spaces that enable iterative collaborative creativity. Creativity researcher Keith Sawyer argued that this design was evidence of the power of collaborative creativity. He said, 'The space aligns with Apple's iterative, improvisational creative process–one where the ideas and designs emerge from collaboration, not from the mind of a brilliant lone genius.'[9] This collaborative creativity has been instrumental in Apple's success. For organizations, the realization that creativity is a shared, collaborative and iterative process is central to their creative process. Of course, a great kitchen does not mean you are a great cook and we have seen organizations spend small fortunes on things (furniture, infrastructure, fittings and buildings) and forget that real change is only possible when you change the culture. Creativity is more than things, it is an attitude of mind and is inherent in re-imagined practices. The next step is to understand that creativity requires discipline.

Myth 3: Creativity is formless and unstructured

Another persistent myth is that creativity is discipline-free and unstructured. Creativity requires discipline and resilience to withstand the iterations and re-iterations required as the project is being developed or when things do not work as planned. For instance, when writers are attempting their first novel, their early drafts are often uninspired and in some cases unreadable. The key to enhancing the writing is to go back and work/re-work or iterate/re-iterate. This is a classic process of learning through trial and error, or put more brutally through abundant failure and intermittent success. This iteration process is hard work but eventually, through drafting and re-drafting the writing and using the writer's skill, produces a novel that an audience will engage with. The author of the international bestseller *The Book Thief*, Marcus Zusak, argues 'Failure has been my best friend as a writer. It tests you, to see if you have what it takes to see it through.'[10]

The products of early creativity are often, initially at least, clichéd and plodding but the potential for creativity is enhanced when organizations are able to develop a climate that celebrates and encourages creative risk-taking that makes imagination, resilience, iteration and playing with possibility commonplace. We often hear leaders arguing that 'risk-taking' is essential but in practice many organizations are deeply risk averse. Acceptance of failure and ultimately risk is difficult for most organizations. Many organizations have a culture of compliance which means risk-taking is avoided and even actively discouraged. This leads to situations where risks are never taken and innovation becomes almost impossible. We are not suggesting that thoughtless and unwise risk taking should become part of any organization's culture. There are, however, wise approaches to risk that encourage creative collaborations and make team-based iteration part of a productive and agile organizational culture.

These myths about creativity matter because they shape attitudes and behaviour and lead to people claiming that they are 'not creative'. If people believe these myths it ultimately means they have no confidence in their own capacity to be creative and as such they cannot make a creative contribution to organizations. If we believe creativity is essential to understanding and solving the challenges that face organizations and our communities, we need to bust these myths. A realistic and deep understanding and active engagement with creativity will make our organizations more dynamic and nimble. The final and most damaging myth of them all is that creativity can not be taught.

Myth 4: Creativity cannot be taught or developed

If creativity is part of some life lottery and our future depends on creativity, we may be in a great deal of trouble. If you believe this myth, you are born with creativity because in some way you are special. Thankfully in our experience this is not the case. Even though we do find many people who believe creativity is a kind of genetic inheritance, we see creativity being established and developed in diverse organizations including jails, big corporates and NGOs. Chen and Kauffman argue that 'creativity has been described as the most important economic resource of the 21st century'.[11] If indeed it is so critical to our economic survival and wellbeing, we are in trouble if creativity is only 'gifted' to a lucky few. Thankfully this is not the case, creativity is an inherency that we are all born with. Of course, like the other skills we are born with, we can chose to learn, develop and strengthen creativity like any other capacity, but it requires hard work and sustained development. As leadership researcher David Burkus argues:

> Our current understanding of genetics leaves us eager to explain away creative ability as coded into someone's genes and thus downplay the creative potential of others ... But the evidence supports a different conclusion. Creative ability isn't limited to a particular personality type, and it isn't controlled by our genetic code. When traditional organizations separate those they think are creative from those they think are not, they are severely limiting their own potential for success.[12]

If we believe creativity is critical in postnormal times we will be working to make it a key capacity in our organizations. This development will require a tangible and implementable approach to creativity such as the Creativity Cascade that we introduce later in this chapter.

Before considering our approach to creativity we would like to explain how we see the interaction between creativity, collaboration, critical reflection and communication. In each of the C chapters (Chapters 4–8) we are going to examine some of the paradoxes we see in their interactions. Paradoxes as discussed in Chapter 3 can deepen our understanding of complexity and contribute to developing wisdom in our approaches. Paradoxes occur where two seemingly oppositional forces (e.g risk and possibility) are present. They are oppositional because risk seems to be in tension with possibility, yet without risk, possibility cannot be created in most organizational settings.

Creativity and the other Cs

Creativity and critical reflection: risk versus possibility

Like so many other human capacities, creativity is neither necessarily good nor evil. There have been multiple occasions throughout history where creativity has been used to deliver oppression, poverty and misery (the risk). For instance, the atomic bomb was an inspired piece of creativity but the pain and suffering it brought on the people of Japan has on-going ramifications internationally. Conversely, many of the great achievements of humanity in architecture, the arts, engineering and science come from recognizing the opportunity that creativity offers. Wisdom, developed through critical reflection (see Chapter 6), brings an ethical dimension to creativity to help individuals and organizations analyse and understand how creativity can be used for productive rather than destructive means.

Additionally, critical reflection opens up questions that relate directly to creativity. In the Dresden Optics' case that opened this chapter, creativity was crucial to imagining a business that had international market appeal. Critical reflection allowed deep analysis of the processes and approaches required to scale Dresden Optics from a start up with one shop to a multinational enterprise.

Creativity and collaboration: individual ingenuity versus collaborative contexts

As we mentioned earlier, creativity in organizations is overwhelmingly a collaborative practice. As creativity researcher Mihaly Csikszentmihalyi argues, 'Creativity does not happen inside people's heads, but in the interaction between a person's thoughts and a socio-cultural context.'[13] While there are individuals who demonstrate high levels of ingenuity, their creative visions require high levels of collaboration for these plans to be realized. Jørn Utzon's original designs for the Sydney Opera House (Figure 5.3(a)) were a wonderful feat of ingenuity but without the team of architects, engineers and builders those plans would have remained marks on paper. In other words, creativity is almost always a collaboration between ideas, people and things. This collaboration makes creative achievements like the Sydney Opera House (Figure 5.3(b)) possible.

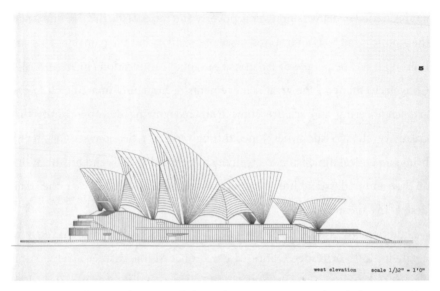

FIGURE 5.3(a) *Utzon's vision of the Sydney Opera House detailed in one of his designs.*

FIGURE 5.3(b) *The Sydney Opera House as it is today.*

Creativity and communication: unknown versus known

To enable deep and rich creative collaboration, organizations and individuals need to clearly and effectively communicate. This kind of communication is challenging because it often demands that individuals and organizations articulate what they had previously only imagined (the unknown). For instance, while an iPhone might be easy to describe now, it was less easy before it existed. The process of developing the breakthrough technologies in the iPhone relied on clear communication of the creative vision of several people from several backgrounds in several different departments within Apple. While the innovation and creativity were critical in the development of the iPhone, none of it would have been possible without high level communication between teams within Apple.

Another aspect of communication and creativity is 'selling the idea'. The term 'cut through' has been used lately (often in politics) to describe clear and effective communication. In a world where there is no shortage of information or media, being able to communicate even the most creative ideas is a profound challenge. In the same way as individuals and organizations need to clearly communicate to support the development of creativity, they also need to understand how to communicate in a crowded marketplace of concepts and ideas. 'Cutting through' requires organizations to clarify their creative process or products with a keen understanding of the audience. More significantly, creativity is about inspiring others with ideas. In this way, the paradox of the unknown and the known are in tension, but must be reconciled to create effective communication.

A process for creativity – the Creativity Cascade

Like all of the 4Cs, creativity is a set of capacities or processes that can be applied to all aspects of organizations. Coherence makers are simply ways of understanding creativity (and the other Cs) so that they can be applied within and across fields of knowledge. We also need to acknowledge that the approach outlined in the Cascade resembles scientific method and other well-known approaches to organizing and making knowledge. This is our intention. We have designed the Cascade and all of the other coherence makers to be applicable as much to the arts as they are to science, economics, business management and engineering.

The Creativity Cascade

In this coherence maker, creativity is imagined as a metaphorical cascade with four stages (or pools) that support creative processes (see Figure 5.4). We are using the cascade metaphor because it suggests a process where one body of water (or understanding) falls (with gravitational force and disciplined but

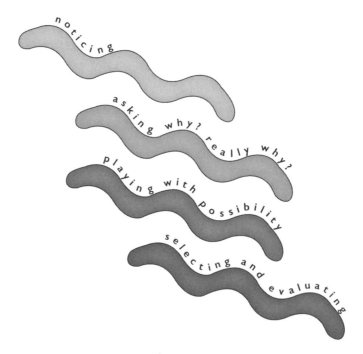

FIGURE 5.4 *The Creativity Cascade.*

varied form) into the next and into the next. The Cascade does not work unless the water flows from one part to the next. The four pools of the Cascade are:

- 🐾 Noticing
- 🐾 Asking why? Really why?
- 🐾 Playing with possibility
- 🐾 Selecting and Evaluating.

The first metaphorical pool of the Cascade is 'noticing'.

Noticing

Educator and philosopher, Maxine Greene described noticing as being able to notice what is there to be noticed.[14] But what does that mean? More recently, writer Martin Lindström popularized the term 'small data' which is a form of noticing. Small data is the noticing of details and patterns such as an 'amalgamation of gestures, habits, likes, dislikes, hesitations, speech patterns, decors, passwords, tweets, status updates and more'.[15] Lindström argues that because of our reliance on big data we are failing to notice, and this has a deep impact on the creative capacities of individuals and organizations.

We think what noticing actually means is that we take the time and energy required not only to perceive but achieve deep and connected perception. Maxine Greene was referring to an art work and Martin Lindström is often noticing consumer behaviour. Irrespective of the context, the principle of noticing is at its core 'a conversation', a concept or an idea where the we can 'nurture appreciative, reflective, cultural, participatory engagement'.[16] For instance, when was the last time you looked really deeply at an image for a long time (say for more than sixty seconds)? If you are anything like us we skip over thousands of images each day without spending any 'noticing' time'. Noticing requires us to become mindful in a process of deep and critical reflection rather than just a series of superficial engagements.

Superficial engagement has been intensified by our screen culture that pushes multiple messages and images into our view on a daily basis. So, given this bombardment it may be possible that as a community and individually we need to learn not only how to notice images and to notice large patterns (big data) but how to notice the small data of relationships, ideas, connections, patterns etc. When we achieve this noticing, it provides the basis for asking deep and informed questions about what we have noticed and the connectedness of the 'noticings' we have achieved. In essence, noticing is a skill that is required for learning (and creativity) but it is rarely discussed and more rarely learnt or taught. To illustrate what noticing looks like we are going to refer to examples from a few different contexts.

Marina Abramović is a New York based performance artist. Her work explores the limitations and possibilities of the body and mind. In a series of recent performances in New York, London and Sydney entitled 'The Artist is Present' (see Figure 5.5) she invites her audience as individuals to

FIGURE 5.5 *Marina Abramović,* The Artist is Present, *Museum of Modern Art, New York, from March 9 to May 31, 2010.*

come in and sit across a table and look at her for as long or as short a time as they liked.

There was a range of experiences from tears to laughter. All of this was consistent with her intention to heighten awareness in the moment. This work is based on the so-called Abramović Method[17] that aims to deepen noticing, sensitivity and perception in the moment. At an installation in Sydney in July 2015 the then CEO of one of Australia's largest banks, Ian Narev, insisted his senior management team attend the performance. His justification for making his executives notice through this work was simple. 'It's very antithetical to the way we lead our day-to-day lives . . .That's what's so valuable about it.'[18]

He wanted his leadership to understand creativity as beginning with noticing so that they could build the capacity into the culture of the bank: 'take any representative collection of 20 CEOs of larger companies, and ask them what worries you most about the capability you lack, I bet creativity will come up in the top three . . . It's really hard because the combination of what we do day to day [in large companies] and creative minds, often doesn't work.'[19] Abramović's work, although seemingly a thousand miles away from management of a multinational bank, is actually central to their creative process. Abramović's process makes each individual slow down and open up their powers of perception, or in other words, their noticing.

In this exercise alone many of the individuals notice their emotions, the way humans interact and the nature of time (small data). In organizations, the same processes can be supported by developing the skills of noticing in a structured and methodical way. Perhaps these activities can be achieved initially through looking deeply into a complex painting, and then listening to a piece of music, and then observing closely and in some detail an interaction between two people. Noticing is the first step in recognizing patterns, seeing relationships and behaviours, and most critically for creativity, provoking curiosity by formulating deep questions about what is being noticed. For organizations, this means noticing the small data as well as the big data. The second metaphorical pool of the Cascade that flows directly from noticing, is asking why and then going deeper to ask, 'really why?'

Asking why? Really why?

If we go back to the Cascade metaphor, there is a flow from noticing to asking why. Curiosity as the basis for deep questioning moves organizations beyond easy answers and invites complex and deeper readings of situations and dilemmas. For example, we could ask the question: 'Why do we struggle to create diverse workplaces?' There are simple answers such as 'because people cannot get on' or perhaps 'because people are intolerant of difference'. While on one level these responses might have some truth to them, they do little to uncover meaning. When we ask 'really why?' we push beyond the first superficial response. 'Asking why? Really why?' searches for deeper answers. These are offered by behavioural economics, psychology, philosophy, sociology, and history. In the instance of diversity in organizations, the 'really why?' question will uncover issues such as racism and stereotyped views about who can do what in an organization, that are deeply cultural. In the 'really why?' phase we are looking for questions that account for or at least acknowledge, the depth and complexity, chaos and contradictions inherent in a problem. The 'really why?' helps to understand problems and issues more deeply. These new understandings can enable re-imagined practices that more effectively deal with the challenge or problem.

We should be wary of the first answer to 'why' because it often reflects a superficial reading of a situation. Rather, we should encourage our individuals and organizations to contemplate the deep questions to enable richer reflection. The aim is to provide time for contemplation and reflection on questions, to encourage deeper and more useful answers. 'Asking why? Really why?' provides time and space to go further and think more deeply. One prime example of another successful entrepreneur who asked really why? is Elon Musk the founder of Tesla, PayPal and SpaceX. He is a modern-day Leonardo da Vinci.

His first major innovation was to make payments on the Internet simple through a start-up company called PayPal, sold for US$1.5 billion to Ebay[20]. Next, Musk bought into a company that makes electric cars feasible and affordable. That car company, Tesla (named after the American innovator) recently had a market capitalization of US$51 billion. He has now built a factory in the Nevada desert that will produce batteries that are designed to replace coal fired power and solve the problem of storing renewable energy (solar and wind).

Elon Musk did not stop there. He is currently working on multi-planetary travel, and an innovative high-speed transport system called the hyperloop where carriages travel in a pressuzised tube that reach speeds of 1,200 km an hour. This would cut the trip from Washington to New York to twenty-nine minutes (the trip currently takes more than three hours by train). Whether these projects are fantastical or probable is not really our point. Our point is creativity requires noticing the gaps and possibilities, and then 'Asking why?' and then 'Really why?' such a thing has not been created. Elon Musk asked why Internet payments were so difficult? Why electric cars were not affordable and widespread? Why batteries for renewable energy were not being mass-produced? He asked why spaceflight was so expensive? He asked why ultra-high-speed land travel was not a reality? While we may not necessarily be able to or even want to replicate Musk's processes in our lives or our organizations, the first two pools of the Creativity Cascade are evident in his radical transport vision. Firstly, noticing a problem and then 'Asking why?' and then 'Really why?' drives innovation, and ultimately solves pressing and real problems. The next pool in the Creativity Cascade is playing with possibility.

Playing with possibility

We have used the term 'playing' rather than 'developing' or 'building' or 'designing' to make the point that possibility and play are critical to creativity.

As adults, play often becomes forgotten in the rush to become 'serious'. That is a great pity because play unlocks possibilities. When we are playing we often throw 'unlike ideas' together to generate new and novel ideas. Playing means improvising in a structured way (which is a bit of a paradox). Play forces people out of their normal constraints and forces them to try sometimes unusual or unexpected approaches that can lead to novel, exciting and ultimately very creative possibilities for organizations and individuals. Complicité is an organization that plays with possibility to make its work.

In 1983 three young entrepreneurial actors, Simon McBurney, Annabel Arden and Marcello Magni,[21] saw the possibility in changing the theatre. They bought an old van for US$700 and performed in scout halls around the United Kingdom performing to growing but modest crowds. That company eventually grew beyond the scout halls and out of the van to become one of the world's most successful international theatre companies. The development of their plays is a process of disciplined play with possibility. As Catherine Alexander

FIGURE 5.6 *Complicité,* A Disappearing Number *rehearsal, 2007.*

suggests. 'The process of devising involves experimenting and discarding numerous ideas, throwing ideas together and allowing the possibility of the unexpected'[22].

Remarkable in Complicité's work is the ceaseless attempt to innovate and change what's possible in the theatre. The possibilities of the performance, text, casting, technology, bodies in space, subject matter – all of this to create theatre like nothing else the world has seen. McBurney says. 'Any play that's making a point is less interesting than something that stays with you and suggests something further'[23]. We have seen several works by this company and what we notice about Complicite's work is the deep connection with possibility. In the play, *A Disappearing Number*, Complicite plays with the seemingly unrelated ideas of 'creativity, the passage of time, memory, cultural divides, and the way in which our past informs our present'[24]. Complicite might seem a long way from our organizations but their performances emerge from an imaginative playing with possibilities based on noticing and 'asking why?' about the world around them and then using these first two pools of the Cascade to play with possibility.

In our view, this process begins with the nurturing of imagination. Imagination is stimulated when people are given time to consider ideas in new ways. For instance, giving teams time to reflect on a business problem by taking them to an unusual setting like a natural history museum or a historic site can disrupt 'business as usual' and stir the imagination. As philosopher Maxine Greene[25] argues: 'Without imagination, you live in a small room with the windows closed. Imagination opens the windows and shows us landscapes, horizons that we would not otherwise perceive.' For her, imagination empowered people to see possibility. Imagination is the first step in the process for playing with possibility. While imagination is predominantly an individual capacity, it feeds the collaborative creative process that is so necessary for innovation. Imagination helps individuals and organizations engage with a range of possibilities that can be shared to build collaborative, creative ideas across expertise domains.

Imagination and collaboration are also critical in the development of possibility thinking. Imagination provides a palate of possibilities for us to explore and play – this is the first step in playing with possibility.

The foundations of the creative process are the skills of noticing and 'asking why?, really why?' Without those two capacities individuals and organizations can potentially be left with an uncontrolled and undisciplined process that does not build knowledge. Playing with possibility builds on these foundations but it can only be productive when the processes of noticing and 'asking why?, really why?' have been understood in a deep and interconnected manner. Playing with possibility is a critical part of the Creativity Cascade, but it is essential for innovation to move to the last part of the Cascade – selecting and evaluating. In this process, we move from 'anything is possible' to 'what will work?'

Selecting and evaluating

The last stage of the Creativity Cascade is selecting and evaluating. In the first part of this stage we consider all the choices that have emerged from playing with possibility. If individuals and organizations have engaged effectively in creative processes, all kinds of choices will have surfaced. At this stage judgement and discernment are required to make choices between all of the possibilities available. For instance, in Dresden Optics' situation that opened the chapter there were several possibilities available for materials production for the frames (see Figure 5.1). Critically they had to select and evaluate from this range of possibilities against the harsh realities of what would sell, and what would work for their processes, and most critically their customers. In the end, they chose a manufacturer close to their retail outlets who could handle recycled plastics and create a durable and inexpensive frame that would keep its costs down.

In Dresden's situation, it was critical for them to keep faith with their potential customers who valued recycling and cost effectiveness, while simultaneously creating a viable business. In this example, and many others, selecting and evaluating is a kind of editing process where we apply wisdom and (prior) knowledge to choose from all of the creative possibilities. At the same time with this choice is an ongoing evaluation. The evaluation process is internal (self-evaluation) and external (listening to the evaluations of others). This phase involves an active process of discernment where we notice the quality of the evaluations. Evaluating requires:

- A self-evaluation that identifies our own assumptions.

- An evaluation from others that critically reflects on the motivations of the evaluator. For instance, what are the assumptions and the agenda of the evaluator?

- A reflection on the quality of the evidence being applied to make the evaluation.

- Consideration of alternative options being suggested through the evaluating process.

This process of evaluation is essential to making creativity transfer effectively to innovation. It is not sufficient to just 'get feedback', we must make selections and seek evaluation from those with understanding of the creative project – someone who 'gets it', engages with it and understands how to enhance the project. Then of course we are back at noticing because unlike a literal cascade we can return to the other pools to develop and extend creative processes. In other words we might toggle between playing with possibility and selecting and evaluating.

Creativity starts with:

- *noticing* – deep perception that flows into asking why, then digging deeper,

- *asking why?, really why?* – asking penetrating complex and connected questions followed by

- *playing with possibility* – imagining and engaging with the palate of possibility, and then finally

🖎 *selecting and evaluating* – which is a process of choice and discernment married with deep and perceptive evaluation (from the individual and from others).

If you have been convinced of the critical place creativity can have in organizations the next step is to consider how we might make creativity a standard expectation for organizations. The concluding parts of this chapter describe the changes we think are necessary to make creativity a standard and predictable reality in the culture of organizations.

Creativity and organizations: getting started

For many, this discussion of creativity will seem like old news. We want to acknowledge that many organizations have been engaging with creativity for decades (see the discussion on Apple earlier). These strategies are for those who can see the potential in creativity but feel that they are not currently meeting that potential. They might also be useful for organizations who have begun the journey but now need to refocus or check their progress.

Questions: A creativity audit

Perhaps the best way to begin, is to look at the opportunities by undertaking a creativity audit using a measure like the Creative Organizations Index[26] or the Situational Outlook Questionnaire.[27] For instance, you might ask the following questions:

- Are our organizations and the units within them prioritising creativity? If not, why not?

- Is there evidence of expertise in different kinds of creativity in the organization?

- Is there evidence the expertise from across the organization is then applied creatively to problems?

- Is imagination and risk-taking encouraged and supported?

- Are there spaces and time in the organization that nurture and support creativity?

Or perhaps you could use the Creativity Cascade to frame your audit. The key questions using the Creativity Cascade are:

- What do we *notice* about the presence or otherwise of creativity in our organization?

- *Why* is this the situation? *Really why*?

- What are the *possibilities* for creativity in our organization?

- How can we *evaluate* change in our organization?

Developing a creative culture in organizations

The second step is reflecting, researching and communicating what worked and what did not. Again, this mostly requires collaboration with partners outside the organization to understand how creative change has occurred, working with professional researchers from universities, consultancy organizations and other places to communicate how to make organizations more creative places. The evidence for creativity and organizations is clear. As we discussed earlier, organizations that feature creativity are more profitable and tend to lead their sectors. With the changes being brought by emerging technologies (such as Artificial Intelligence), individuals, communities and organizations are facing uncertain times. For our organizations to be successful we need to engage with creativity, but more than that, we need to develop frameworks, processes and approaches that make creativity understandable, learnable and able to be practised.

Creativity in our view is critical for organizations to make innovation possible. Without these capacities, our organizations become irrelevant, unprofitable and eventually extinct. If we manage to change our organizations to make them more creative we future proof them and provide new capacities for our community and society to face the imminent super complex challenges that the twenty-first century continues to present.

Getting started: building creativity in organizations

Building authentic creativity requires an organization to ask the following big questions.

How is 4C creativity in your organization:

1 Active and agentic

   Does everyone in the organization have the opportunity to exercise creativity in their role? If not why not?

2 Central

   How can creativity become part of the DNA of your organization instead of a 'nice to have' for some chosen few individuals?

3 Systematic

   How can creativity be integrated into the systems and processes of your organization? If there is a process for creativity (such as the Creativity Cascade), how can it be implemented?

4 Part of the innovation strategy

   If creativity is innovation literacy how is innovation possible without creativity?

5   Collaborative

Is creativity understood as an individual quest for leaders or 'creatives' or is it an expectation that everyone will work together to make it a reality?

In the next chapter, we consider the next of our C's, critical reflection, and how that can support the transformation of individuals and organizations.

6

Critical reflection

Critical reflection is a process to help individuals and organizations understand power, structures and practices. Like creativity, it is often more apparent in its absence rather than its presence. Often when we consider the collapse or near-death experience of an organization this lack of critical reflection becomes

FIGURE 6.1 *A vintage Volkswagen.*

clear. As we will see in the Volkswagen (VW) case and throughout this chapter, critical reflection can often prevent the meltdown of organizations by ensuring members of an organization have time to think deeply and then have agency (appropriate power and ability to speak up and act).

This chapter explores the ways organizations can use critical reflection to make them more effective, satisfying and motivating places to be. When it all goes wrong a lack of critical reflection is often the culprit. In this case we consider the recent failures of critical reflection at VW.

Trouble at Volkswagen

In September 2015 VW admitted that it had fitted devices that distorted emissions in its eleven million diesel vehicles.[1] This scandal, which implicated hundreds of employees from management to workers on the factory floor, had many causes, but perhaps the most serious was the absence of critical reflection and agency in VW's workforce and management. The aggressive and 'no-failure' leadership style and culture at VW, which has been described by commentators and employees as typically 'top down' and featured poor communication, that engendered fear rather than autonomy led to a closed organization (organizations that are not transparent to the outside world). Many critics of VW have attributed the diesel emissions scandal to its authoritarian and closed-off corporate culture. In other words, to a lack of critical reflection within the company.

The potential consequence of an absence of critical reflection within an organization is not trivial. It cost VW US$16.9 billion[2] and incalculable reputational damage. The lesson for us is that companies with autocratic leaders who create passive workforces ultimately pay the price. On the other hand, building critically reflective organizations can pay dividends. As International Business academic Jan Jung argues, critical reflection enables a culture in an organization where everyone feels welcome to share what worked or did not work. This free exchange of information could help the company become more innovative and effectively address new demands in the industry.[3]

In essence, critical reflection provides individuals with the opportunity to analyse organizational processes, practices and approaches so they can understand 'how things work', where the power is held and through this understanding how change might occur to achieve transformation. Critical reflection allows individuals within organizations to be 'awake' to their own agency and power, and how the power and agency of others affects them. Before we consider the evidence for the usefulness of critical reflection, lets define what we actually mean by it.

What is critical reflection?

Critical reflection provides individuals and organizations with the capacity to understand power and the way it is exercised. It provides an understanding of how to navigate and have agency in complex systems (like most of the organizations we work or interact with), rather than creating organizations full of passive individuals or, at worst victims. Critical reflection uncovers tensions, contradictions and illogical features of organizations. When critical reflection is implemented it can bring to the surface 'the emotions and politics that are part of the underlying assumptions and expectations that inform everyday practice.'[4] When these relationships are 'surfaced' it is then possible to change practices with the assumptions now open for all to see. When added to the other three Cs, critical reflection offers individuals and organizations ways to understand how their own assumptions and backgrounds influence knowledge. They can also understand that knowledge is inherently dynamic, contested and contestable. This has the potential to build organizations that are engaging and dynamic places where knowledge as learning is used effectively to create transformation.

As we discussed in Chapter 4, successful organizations are or become successful through their capacity to learn, and, through that learning, grow. In this chapter, we would like to explain how critical reflection makes that learning possible. We are going to start with a case study of a small organization (that we are involved with) in an everyday situation.

Case study: Critical reflection, negotiation and lessons learnt

3D Learning (3DL) is a small start-up in the educational services and organizational change space. In its establishment phase the organization was very small and had only one employee but employed several sub-contractors to work with organizations (corporations, NGOs, small businesses, schools, universities and other organizations) to build transformation through learning programmes and mentoring. The business had no venture capital, apart from the time the founders had contributed to the establishment of the company. In many ways, this organization is no different to any other in any sector except that the founders were (and still are) attempting to build the company on principles consistent with the 4Cs and particularly critical reflection.

In the first few months of the company's existence an opportunity emerged to work with a high-profile organization (in this case study we will refer to it as Calipron[5]). 3DL (even from the start) suggested that the relationship should be negotiated where the assumptions on each side were clear. 3DL also wanted to ensure that Calipron and 3DL were able to develop the most efficient and productive relationship given the uneven power situation between them. At the first meeting with Calipron, even though this expectation was discussed, Calipron insisted on certain ways of working which reverted to a service provider/client relationship. 3DL was at that stage just getting on its feet and the opportunity to work with a client in the sector provided opportunities for 'word of mouth' and further growth with similar clients – it was a big break. 3DL normally resisted this approach because its best and most productive work occurred when relationships were collaborative, rather than the more familiar 'client to service provider' approach.

Calipron insisted on 'bolt on' solutions rather than a more negotiated approach that included mentoring and leadership development with incremental professional learning across the business over twelve months. The outcome was less than satisfactory for all involved. The power relationship ensured that Calipron did not have effective experiences and 3DL was not able to support effective transformation in that context. There were some positives, as Calipron did make some progress through the arrangement, but the relationship never met the potential for true transformation.

In other contexts, and other sites, the 3DL's approach is negotiated. When that occurs, the power relationships are understood and expectations are set effectively at the outset. In this instance, if critical reflection had been the basis for the relationship, assumptions would have been identified early. This kind of analysis goes beyond critical thinking. In critical reflection, organizations must consider the human-scale processes at work (power, emotion, status, motivations) and then apply those understandings to a relationship or a set of relationships. To analyse what went wrong in this situation let us first look at the stages of critical reflection that we will discuss later in this chapter as part of the Critical Reflection Crucible coherence maker. The first is *identifying assumptions*.

Identifying assumptions

What were 3DL's assumptions and what assumptions did 3DL have about Calipron? What expectations were set by Calipron? What opportunities were there for negotiation both ways? What assumptions were there on both sides about the site and the need for transformation? Often individuals and organizations begin new projects and new relationships without surfacing their assumptions. Sometimes these assumptions are not even conscious. This process allows a clear understanding of the conscious and unconscious assumptions and biases we hold about any given situation. If this forms part of the initial conversations it can 'clear the air' and set up a more realistic understanding for each party to move forward.

Why this? why so?

Having identified assumptions, the organizations could have explored the why? of their assumptions. For instance: Why do I believe what I believe about this site? Why is it so that the community holds different beliefs to the beliefs and assumptions I hold? Calipron held several assumptions that impeded transformation. In this instance, Calipron believed it had already made significant progress towards 4C transformation, but there was insufficient time given to considering how the human-scale processes had changed. For instance, had the power relationships shifted? Was the climate for risk-taking changed? Was the fear that had driven so much decision making altered at all? Calipron assumed they had, but 3DL could only see incremental change. These questions could have prompted questions from both 3DL and Calipron to seek clarification around these assumptions, and to understand why these assumptions about change were held so strongly by Calipron (*why this? why so?*). In the next phase, which is the negotiation phase, a discussion could have begun around what was going to work based on the assumptions that had been discussed earlier.

Contesting, elaborating and adapting

In the stage *contesting, elaborating and adapting*, assumptions are investigated against the evidence. Deep and true collaboration is achieved through careful negotiation that is informed by critical reflection. In 3DL's case the assumptions about change readiness of Calipron could have been contested, evidence could have been discussed and a more informed analysis could have supported the on-going relationship. Emerging from the evidence and bringing to bear the skills of 3DL, the partnership could have adapted, negotiated and delivered an effective co-created transformation program that built on mutual strengths. This final phase in critical reflection is what we call *re-solving*.

Re-solving

In this phase, the organization considers the assumptions that contestation, elaboration and adaptions provide and reconfigure (re-solve) organizational practices to create a more effective and more evidence-based approach to creating achievable transformation. In this situation, none of these approaches were enacted. While not a total disaster the situation did leave both 3DL and Calipron unsatisfied.

We have cited this seemingly unremarkable case study because these situations occur more frequently than the large and dramatic situations in organizations (such as the VW emissions scandal that opened this chapter) that result from a lack of critical reflection.

There are of course more serious examples, such as the high-profile actors and movie producers that misused their power to sexually assault their co-workers. Or we could have discussed the many cases where people in educational, community, business, NGO or religious organizations have abused their power and exploited and damaged the vulnerable. In some ways the small cases and the large cases make a similar point, which is that unchallenged assumptions stemming from poor or non-existent critical reflection on organizational processes and structures often leads to distortions in those organizations. In serious cases this can produce damage to vulnerable people affected by the power imbalance, such as workers, clients, students or congregants. Getting the relationships right through transparent and deeply integrated critical reflection can avoid these issues and lead to true organizational transformation.

As an organization, we learnt that when critical reflection is ignored or downplayed in relationships it has implications for that relationship. For us, this learning has guided our commitment to critical reflection and developing relationships that are carefully negotiated. Lets first make clear what we mean by critical reflection by exploring what 'critical' means when related to critical reflection.

What is so 'critical' about reflection?

Critical[6] reflection allows individuals and organizations to stand 'one step back' and analyse (question) knowledge in terms of power and agency (an individual's sense of control). By knowledge we mean all of the 'knowings' of an organization including process 'knowings', relationship 'knowings', market 'knowings' and so on. By agency we mean the ability for individuals to work wisely, ethically and autonomously according to their free will rather than blindly accepting the will of others. German sociologist, Jurgen Habermas argues that critically reflective knowledge allows deep learning. He claims 'critical reflective knowledge is neither behavioural nor technical, not truth establishing nor captured by a discipline. It critiques all other forms of knowledge, and in so doing, it moves beyond merely reproducing what is'[7]. Critical reflection allows for deep questioning that inquires about different knowings and the connections between them.

For organizations considering transformation, critical reflection helps us to analyse knowledge. For instance, when studying organizational processes (such as the negotiations between 3DL and Calipron) critical reflection seeks to perceive and surface the power relationships and the implications of those relationships on others. If individuals and organizations are unable to understand power in their own context, they can start with external examples such as the case studies we present here to analyse the relationships at 'one step removed' (this often removes the 'noise' that emerges when analysing your own situation).

Before we move more deeply into what critical reflection is through further exploration of the Critical Reflection Crucible coherence maker, let us first unpack some of the myths about critical reflection.

Myths of critical reflection

Myth 1: Critical reflection is self-indulgent

The common misconception is that reflection occurs in isolation and leads to contemplation ('navel gazing' rather than action). On the contrary, critical reflection when it works most effectively leads to deep and transformative action. It develops as we collaborate and gain a deep understanding of how organizations create, communicate and collaborate to deliver effectively for their community, customers or in their markets (or wherever they operate). Fundamentally, critical reflection relies on a deep and broad analysis that makes transparent each individual's assumptions. This is not intended to paralyse thinking but rather to contextualize these ideas, expose the individual to evidence and seek to build new collective, collaborative and creative approaches to change. When this is successful these ideas do not remain ideas, they are enacted to make transformation possible. In essence, critical reflection leads to more informed, transparent and therefore better decision making.

Myth 2: Critical reflection is subjective and therefore not useful

Critical reflection is based on our own impressions and ideas but it cannot stop there. Critically, it tests our assumptions to ensure that subjectivity is informed and evidence-based. Subjectivity emerges from your own judegments and objectivity can be verified by more than one person as 'factual'. For instance, you might subjectively decide that a painting is not high quality because of its themes and the style in which it is painted (such as expressionist, surrealist, naturalist). Objectively we could argue that the painting is 350 mm × 450 mm, uses twenty-six colours and depicts sunflowers. Of course, both objectivity and subjectivity have their place in organizations. We are not arguing here or anywhere in this book that subjectivity is a problem and objectivity is the answer. We argue that subjectivity needs to be accounted for and understood in organizations and individuals. We need to make those subjectivities apparent and test them with each other.

Critical reflection researchers Fook, White and Gardner argue[8] subjectivity is critical to organizational learning as long as it is transparent. As they claim: 'Being reflexive by taking into account subjectivity will involve a knowledge of who I am as a whole being (social, emotional, physical, cultural, economic, political) and understanding the effects this has on the knowledge I perceive and create'[9]. Here subjectivity is not discouraged, rather it is considered a critical part of the process of assessing and understanding processes and approaches in work and life. In a 'post fact' world where truths have lost their currency, critical reflection on our own subjectivities becomes even more critical. Subjectivities that are based on untested assumptions such as 'it's OK to cheat on emissions standards' can have catastrophic results (as the VW example demonstrates). While there is a subjective judgement, it is not a judgement based on effective critical reflection or wisdom.

Myth 3: Critical reflection does not lead to action

Critical reflection is suited to the 4Cs because it is inherently collaborative and interactive and when effective leads to transformation. As Fook and colleagues argue: 'In this sense, critical reflection involves social and political analyses which enable transformative changes, whereas reflection may remain at the level of relatively undisruptive changes in techniques or superficial thinking.'[10] If critical reflection is to be effective it cannot remain just an individual reflective process, it must lead to creative, communicative and collaborative action. This action can be challenging for organizations as action often leads to the questioning of existing structures and practices, and will present at least three tensions.

'[F]irst, there will be a tension between what is revealed in public and what remains in private.'[11] While some personal matters must remain confidential it is crucial that organizations are open and honest about transformation processes. In our view, this open recognition is a demonstration of strength – it says to the world 'our company is open about needing to change and ask the hard questions'. In the case of VW, the cover-up and the secrecy compounded the difficulty for the organization.

The second tension arises between the imperatives of organizational success/ survival and the well-being of organizational members. This tension is felt deeply by those leading and those engaging in transformation. The hard truth is people move on in transformation. Sometimes the separation is mutually beneficial but sometimes, as we all know, it is not. Organizations that articulate the vision and the roadmap for transformation often alleviate that problem as team members who cannot see themselves in the transformation 'move on'.

The third tension Fook nominates is between reflection that leads to changes in practice and reflection that maintains the status quo. Reflection that does not extend beyond the status quo risks being inherently superficial, self-indulgent and disconnected from the world. Real critical reflection that turns into influential communication can make transformation more than a 'bunch of ideas'.

Myth 4: Critical reflection and critical thinking are the same

Even though it shares the term 'critical' with critical thinking, critical reflection is qualitatively different. Critical thinking is, as researchers Scriven and

Paul suggest, 'the intellectually disciplined process of actively and skilfully conceptualizing, applying, analyzing, synthesizing, and/or evaluating information gathered from, or generated by, observation, experience, reflection, reasoning, or communication, as a guide to belief and action'.[12] You may notice that many of the features of critical thinking are found in our coherence makers for creativity, communication and collaboration. The steps of noticing, asking why? and then really why? in the Creativity Cascade discussed in Chapter 5 are inherent in critical thinking. In critical reflection those 'understandings' are revisited and disrupted so that the assumptions that underpin our knowledge and learning are not left unchallenged. Rather, the process of critical reflection helps individuals and organizations to understand that knowledge and the application of knowledge is frequently contested and contestable. Critical reflection is a crucial part of positioning knowledge in organizations, analysing and critiquing it to build an understanding of the ways knowledge, context and power actively and dynamically co-exist and interact.

Myth 5: Critical reflection is cost free

While critical reflection may sound like a soft, 'nice to have' quality, real and active critical reflection will cost organizations in time, money and energy. It is, however, a cost that is more of an investment. Critical reflection will necessarily disrupt the structures, processes and practices of organizations and will directly question how power is created and exercised throughout. As Fook and and colleagus argue:

> managers are right to be skeptical about the value of reflection if they only think of their role is ensuring stability and order, or if they imagine that it is their duty to guarantee what the company wants, no matter what it takes. Employees, at times, also rightly feel that the experience of being 'empowered' by reflection, and therefore being more visible or vocal in the organization, can have unwanted and sometimes painful consequences.[13]

Critical reflection involves radical transparency. This approach is inherently disruptive and for some organizations deeply countercultural. There is, however, a potentially catastrophic cost of doing 'business as usual' – a cost that can lead to the demise of organizations. The case studies in this chapter have demonstrated there is the cost of doing nothing, but there is also a cost to developing critical reflection in organizations. Let's turn now to the evidence that critical reflection actually works.

The evidence for critical reflection

In a recent summary of the research into critical reflection, Jan Fook and colleagues discovered strong benefits for individuals and communities including:

- empowerment,
- increased competence and confidence,
- capacity to deal with uncertainty,
- increased capacity to manage emotional turmoil and stress,
- the ability to work better in teams with colleagues,
- the capacity to integrate theory and practice, and
- being able to plan actions.[14]

If these claims are true it begs the question: Why is critical reflection not central and mandatory for all organizations? It seems to us that the answer lies in the costs that critical reflection brings to established power structures' ways of doing things. If organizations engage with critical reflection (and that is not an easy decision for most) deliberate strategies are required. The development of these strategies will necessarily involve the interactions with communication, focused creativity and trusting collaboration.

Critical reflection and the 4Cs: the paradoxes

As we have discussed throughout this book, the 4Cs interact with each other in the processes and structures of organizations. High quality critical reflection creates an organizational climate where creativity, collaboration and communication can flourish. The paradoxes we outline in these chapters identify seeming contradictions that when looked at more closely actually intersect and interact. In other words we may think that our agency (ability to control) and at the same time undergo challenge, are contradictory. When we look at this more closely, challenge helps us clarify our questions. Critical reflection makes this possible because it generates a readiness to consider preconceptions and assumptions and to develop ways of working that are analytical. Here are the ways we see this happening in organizations.

Critical reflection and collaboration: agency versus challenge

One of the critical reflection myths we discussed earlier is that it is individual and self-indulgent. Jan Fook's work with social workers models a collaborative critical reflection approach. Rather than seeing critical reflection as an individual activity she maintains the process should be central to how we create a dynamic and vibrant culture in our organizations. In essence, it comes from the agency of the individual, but relies on fundamental change as individuals collaborate to change organizational culture. For instance, in an organization like Dresden Optics (Chapter 5) we saw an individual in Bruce Jeffreys who could ask searching deep questions about the market for eyewear and eye health generally. However, for him to answer these questions, he needs the skills and capacities of many to collaborate with him. Fook sees critical reflection as a way to understand the whole rather than all of the parts. She says, 'For me, it is about investigating someone's holistic (incorporating beliefs, emotions, and meaning) experience (through critical reflection) in a way that not only helps them learn from it anew, but also helps them learn how to learn from it'.[15] She claims that critical reflection is not only about considering one's assumptions and predispositions to a given idea, but it also invites us to consider knowledge in the light of a deep understanding of not only our own personal position, but also how our personal position relates to that new idea and to others.

This process becomes necessarily collaborative when we think about the ways knowledge is created in the 4Cs – not as an isolated and self-indulgent process but rather as a co-construction that respects diversity, but also acknowledges (and often celebrates) subjectivities. For instance, if an individual working in a policy role is considering refugee policy they may have a set of assumptions on these issues. As they critically reflect with colleagues, the process will expose their assumptions to evidence and differing views. In an authentic critical reflection process, each individual's assumptions are challenged in a group discussion, so all involved are prompted to analyse their subjectivities with questions such as: Who makes decisions about citizenship? Who has the right to be a citizen? Who does not have the right to be a citizen? What role does refugee status play in the rights to citizenship? This way of working opens up new spaces for dialogue and ensures that subjectivities are analysed and often challenged. This approach models broader democratic processes rather than isolating individuals to work things out on their own.

In practice, there are two phases to critical reflection. The first phase is inherently individual. This process prompts the individual to consider knowledge in the light of their conscious and unconscious assumptions and preconceptions. But the work of reflection does not stop there. If organizations are to be effective, individuals must work with each other to support critical reflection by respectfully testing each other's assumptions. Not as a destructive process but as a way of understanding difference and creating a kind of creative dissonance – a space for a variety of views that can bump up against each other.

Critical reflection is an inherently and necessarily collaborative process. While critical reflection may begin at an individual level, it must engage collaboratively with others to become effective. For transformation to take hold in organizations, reflective practice needs to engage critically, creatively and collaboratively with others to transform one's own practice and in so doing transform the practice of the broader organization.

Critical reflection and creativity: unlearning versus new learning

In the Creativity Cascade (Chapter 5) we identified two critical components of creative learning – 'noticing' and 'asking why?, really why?'. The unlearning we do in critical reflection helps to challenge old 'learnings', and when faced with new or shifting information, create new understandings. The *Cambridge Dictionary* defines unlearning as 'to make an effort to forget your usual way of doing something so that you can learn a new and sometimes better way'.[16] As part of the noticing process we should perceive the ways we respond to different kinds of ideas. Flowing from this noticing should be a series of 'why' questions that consider our preconceptions and assumptions and the ways these assumptions form our attitudes. For instance, we might notice that our colleagues have strong responses to discussions around change in the workplace. If they are critically reflective they will then ask 'why' this response? Of course, the first response might be 'I hate change'. When they become more critically reflective (ask really why?) they will move beyond their initial why questions and begin to understand this attitude may be formed by unchallenged views about change or negative prior experiences. Once these assumptions and experiences are unpacked and understood, individuals and organizations can play with possibility to discover that change has many components and can take many forms (some deeply negative and some quite positive) which has the potential to radically change the culture of organizations.

Critical reflection and communication: interpreting versus messaging

Critical reflection allows us to listen, understand, interpret and then create messages. The deep questions inherent in critical reflection facilitates a connection between listening and creating messages so both can be deepened. Critical reflection makes us 'alert to messaging' so we *understand* the text, the context and subtext of the communication as we make it and receive it. Communication relies on individuals being able to clearly articulate not only a message but to understand what motivates their views and assumptions. This creates in individuals a kind of meta-awareness of communication strategies. Critical reflection enables us to think more deeply and understand the genesis of our views and to test those views against other knowledge and opinion. As Jack Mezirow argues, in creating communication, reflection helps us to make messages that are resistant to distortion and presupposition:

> To make meaning means to make sense of an experience; we make an interpretation of it. When we subsequently use this interpretation to guide decision making or action, then making meaning becomes learning. … Reflection enables us to correct distortions in our beliefs and errors in problem solving. Critical reflection involves a critique of the presuppositions on which our beliefs have been built.[17]

Mezirow argues here that critically reflecting helps us to unearth distortions and to critique what we think we know. As we make meaning in our communication and attempt to convey that meaning to others, critical reflection enables us to seek clarity and to understand how our subjectivities influence our communication strategies. This approach makes the 'subtexts' of communication clear, leaving less room for noise and confusion. A critically reflective communicator can analyse and clarify their own meaning making and analyse the communication strategies and approaches of others. Having considered the place of critical reflection in the 4Cs we would now like to introduce our coherence maker for critical reflection: the Critical Reflection Crucible.

The Critical Reflection Crucible coherence maker

As with the other three Cs, we are committed to providing a model for how critical reflection can be understood and enacted in organizations. In this coherence maker, we imagine critical reflection as a crucible. We have used the metaphor of the crucible to emphasize the need to test and 'fire' knowledge against the heat of our reflections and the reflections of others. The metaphorical crucible ensures that what emerges is not tainted with non-essential materials but rather has integrity. The heavy and industrial nature of the analogy (the crucible) is deliberate. Reflection has often been dismissed as a 'soft skill' but in

FIGURE 6.2 *The Critical Reflection Crucible.*

reality it is difficult and demanding. As we discussed, critical reflection is so demanding that it is rarely apparent in organizations. We see the critical reflection (through the analogy of the crucible) as a heavy, rigorous and difficult process that requires skill and effort to create ideas that will withstand and will be supported by scrutiny.

As with the other coherence makers we have identified, the crucible is not the only way to understand critical reflection, it is, however, one way of visualizing a structure that can be used as we consider how we build and transform organizations. The Critical Reflection Crucible does not seek equilibrium in knowledge. Rather, it recognizes that knowledge is complex, influenced by our own subjectivities and that it remains dynamic as the context and situations change around organizations. As knowledge is created new layers and connections emerge as understanding grows. So, equilibrium is not always possible or even desirable. We prefer the analogy of a crucible where fire refines and tests knowledge to make it resilient, strong and transparent. The phases of the Critical Reflection Crucible are:

- Identifying assumptions
- Why this? Why so?
- Contesting, elaborating and adapting
- Re-solving.

A process for critical reflection: the Critical Reflection Crucible

Identifying assumptions

We all come with our own subjectivities that are sometimes conscious but frequently unconscious (these might also include unconscious bias). Often these assumptions are not based on evidence or an understanding of how evidence relates to those assumptions. We have nominated 'identifying assumptions' as this makes clear to individuals and organizations that every individual has assumptions about knowledge (some might call this 'baggage'). To move beyond these assumptions, we need to understand how our views are created and how they might be re-created.

We are going to return to discussions around climate change to explain how the Critical Reflection Crucible might work in practice. Climate change is useful in understanding critical reflection, as individuals often approach this topic with a series of opinions and attitudes that have not been challenged or tested with evidence. Like any set of beliefs these views could have been formed by work colleagues, family, friends or the media but may not have been the product of deep and reflective consideration of the complexity and evidence around this topic.

The process of critical reflection invites us to develop understanding by contrasting our views against the evidence to understand not only the issues of critical reflection but also the nature of the discipline. In science, a key part of scientific process is scientific method. If we understand that findings are developed through this disciplined process it provides us with not only an appreciation of the issue (climate change) but also the processes of how knowing is created in science itself. This allows individuals to untangle the meaning separating opinion from evidence. The ability to untangle knowledge is a critical skill for individuals and organizations facing the complexity, chaos and contradictions of the modern world. For this stage of the crucible we should be exploring the following questions:

- What does our organization believe?
- Who gains from this belief?
- How have those beliefs been formed?
- Are those beliefs and assumptions based on evidence? What is the evidence?

- How can individuals and organizations rethink their beliefs as they become aware of new knowledge and evidence?

Equally the ability to understand our assumptions and approaches to knowledge also lays the foundation for the next feature of the Crucible: Why this? why so?

Why this? Why so?

Once we have understood the subjectivities we bring, and untangled the different aspects of a given problem, the next step is to ask 'why' questions that clarify our reflections. In this phase of the coherence maker we are also considering where the status and power lies in the situation. In other words, who gains and who loses here?

Similar to the Creativity Cascade, this phase requires questioning that prompts us to seek contextual and 'joined up' understanding of knowledge. If we return to the climate change question we might ask ourselves and others (potentially including external climate experts/consultants):

- Why do I hold the views on climate change that I hold? (Why so?)
- Why is climate change receiving such prominence in the media? (Why this?)
- Why do people disagree on the causes of climate change? (Why so?)

This kind of questioning develops an understanding that knowledge is contested, connected across disciplines, and contextual. The 'why this?', 'why so?' phase of the Crucible encourages individuals to think deeply about the knowledge that is confronting them. For some individuals, this may be provocative as it disrupts many of the assumptions they have made about knowledge and 'knowing'. Ultimately this leads to a stronger connection with the nature of knowledge and not just the issue itself, and builds an individual's (and ultimately an organization's) capacity to contest, elaborate and adapt knowledge, having asked key questions about the nature and content of that knowledge.

In the 'why this? why so?' phase of the Critical Reflection Crucible the following questions may arise:

- Why is this knowledge being promoted above other knowledge?

- Who is promoting this knowledge and why?

- How does this knowledge connect with other parts of knowledge?

- Who gets to tell the story about this knowledge? And why?

At this point, we are ready to engage in the next phase of the Critical Reflection Crucible: contesting, elaborating and adapting.

Contesting, elaborating and adapting

As we discussed at the beginning of this chapter, critical reflection is often dismissed as a kind of self-indulgent and endless 'navel-gazing'. Our view of critical reflection encourages action and collaboration rather than contemplation alone. At the contesting, elaborating and adapting stage, ideas and knowledge are tested (or fired) to elaborate preliminary concepts and then adapt them to other problems or domains of knowledge. Returning to the climate change example, once individuals and organizations understand the nature of scientific evidence they are then equipped to contest scientific 'fact' using scientific method. Given the rules of the discipline they can now understand how they have been influenced by their subjectivities, how evidence is used in science to make findings and how the test–retest principle might be applied to contest that knowledge. Perhaps more usefully they now have the knowledge to make extensions and elaborations to arguments about climate change and climate science that relate directly to their role in the organization. For instance, for those working in insurance a deep and critical understanding of evidence around climate change will support sound business decisions about risks and costs for premiums. This process is not just about thinking. Contesting, elaborating and adapting necessarily involves re-imaging practices and approaches as a result of the critical reflection process. Critical reflection positions knowledge as dynamic, adaptable, malleable and actionable, much like the molten liquid inside a crucible. The liquid in a crucible does not remain liquid permanently. Some questions that might be useful to frame understanding at this stage of the Critical Reflection Crucible are:

- How does this knowledge conflict or agree with other available evidence?

- How can this knowledge be enhanced in the light of new evidence?

- How can this knowledge be adapted to new contexts or circumstances?

The next feature of the Critical Reflection Crucible is re-solving.

Re-solving

The term re-solving describes the active re-formulation of ideas. This occurs after:

- testing assumptions,

- asking critical questions,

- contesting the knowledge, and then

- viewing that knowledge as dynamic to be elaborated and applied before settling on a view or approach.

In our view, knowledge may become firm but it is never completely solid, so the process of re-solving always accounts for the remaking and the re-application of knowledge in new circumstances and contexts. In our climate change example individuals may re-solve a position based on climate science evidence that sea level rises will have certain effects on small Pacific islands such as Tuvalu. If at a later stage the initial projections understate the sea level rises, we can then re-solve this projection through a series of recalculations and take action based on that re-solved knowledge. The process is not passive but interactive, collaborative and engaged with the evidence and expertise that has become available. Key questions for this phase of that Critical Reflection Crucible include:

- How can this area of knowledge be connected to other ideas to create new knowledge?

- What is the impact of this knowledge in different contexts? Is this knowledge context dependent? What does not work across contexts?

- What factors could influence and change this knowledge in the future?

- Who has the most to gain from this knowledge?

Like all of the 4C coherence makers we have described, the process is not linear and features of the Crucible overlap, occur simultaneously or become re-arranged depending on the circumstances and contexts. What does not shift, however, is the need for individuals and organizations to understand that knowledge is complex. Critical reflection provides an approach that conceptualizes knowledge as dynamic, connected and influenced by individual preconceptions.

Critical reflection starts with:

- *Identifying assumptions* – identifying uncontested ideas which may impede progress.

- *Why this? Why so?* – asking mindful and critical questions that lead to the contesting, elaborating and adapting of action to re-solve issues and respond to challenges and opportunities.

- *Contesting, elaborating and adapting* – asking penetrating complex and connected questions that allow for discussion, dissonance and change of views, structures, strategies and culture.

- *Re-solving* – re-creating structures, strategies and cultures that reflect effective evidence based practice and respect all participants individual agency.

Critical reflection for flourishing

In an editorial in *Reflective Practice* in 2010 researcher Tony Ghaye[18] asks the question: 'In what ways can reflective practices enhance human flourishing?' He wonders whether reflective practice can help humans: 'bounce back from adverse events in our lives? Would they help us be more open-minded, have more creative thoughts, enjoy better relationships with others, be more resilient?' While there is still no definitive answer to this question there are increasing signs that critical reflection is beneficial and may be necessary to face the complex challenges that lie ahead.

If we believe that human flourishing is part of what organizations aspire to, critical reflection should be at the heart of how organizations create ways of knowing and doing. Jan Fook and colleagues claim that: '... there is a mounting body of well-researched claims about the benefits and outcomes of critical reflection, and that these on the whole are consistent and supportive of each other. There are contributions to "human flourishing".'[19] Critical reflection has a role to play in helping all of us (individuals, organizations, leaders and communities) to test our motivations and understandings before taking action. In acting or doing we contest, elaborate and adapt to respond to challenges and to do better. If we can achieve this in our organizations we may contribute to human flourishing rather than human disintegration.

Getting started: building critical reflection in organizations

Building authentic critical reflection requires an organization to ask the following big questions.

How is 4C critical reflection in your organization:

1   Active and agentic

    How does the organization's critical reflection allow evidence to support decision making rather than power structures?

2   Central

    How can critical reflection change work practices and culture in your organization?

3   Connected

    How can critical reflection be in structures and connect strategies, processes and approaches in your organization?

4   Cultural

    How can critical reflection change unhelpful, ineffective or damaging practices or processes in your organization?

5   Reform-focussed

    How can critical reflection lead to the reform of organizational cultures to make them more satisfying and effective?

In the next chapter, we explore how action can follow from critical reflection through empowered communication.

7

Communication

How do you re-imagine a visit to the cinema in Peru? Cineplanet, Peru's largest cinema chain asked themselves this question in 2014 and approached the international design firm IDEO to help them solve it. IDEO design not only objects, they design tools, conversations, experiences and environments that help organizations to innovate and change. This is the 'design thinking' that Cineplanet knew they needed as an organization to keep ahead of the game. They knew they not only had to re-imagine the movie-going experience, they

FIGURE 7.1 *Re-imagining the cinema experience.*

had to re-imagine their thinking as an organization to change. This chapter uses IDEO's collaboration with Cineplanet as a case study to illustrate the key role 'true communication' plays not only in innovation but in the transformation of organizations.

A case study in communication (and the other Cs) – IDEO and Cineplanet

The story begins with Cineplanet in 1998 when three Peruvian friends, after finishing their MBAs in the USA, decided to return to their home country to establish a start-up. They noticed the number of movie goers had declined in Peru from fifteen million in 1981 to three million in 1995 and realized their country's entertainment sector was significantly under-serviced. With the resolution of civil unrest in the 1990s and 2000s, and the growth of an emerging middle class, families felt safe and financially secure enough to begin going to concerts, sporting events and cinemas. Going to the movies has now become one of the favourite pastimes for Peruvians, and the number of cinema customers doubled between 2006 and 2012. Cineplanet quickly became the largest cinema company in Peru and is a leader in technology and service innovation in the Peruvian cinema industry.

Despite Cineplanet's success as market leaders and innovators, they did not want to fall into the trap of video rental retailer Blockbuster. Cineplanet's CEO, Fernado Soriano, explained: 'We are doing extremely well, and this is exactly the time when we should invest. Look at Blockbuster. They didn't invest in their company when things were good and they went out of business. We don't want the same thing to happen to us.'[1] Cineplanet wanted to move from making decisions based on assumptions of what customers wanted from an operations point of view, to focusing on what customers really wanted in the cinema experience. In 2014 Cineplanet chose to work with design company IDEO, as they knew the 'redesign' had to be more than introducing new products and services, it had to implement more profound cultural change within the company. Mildreth Maldonado, the CFO of Cineplanet, claimed: 'This is not a one-time project. It's just the beginning of something new inside the firm.'[2]

IDEO is known for its' human-centred, 'empathic' approach to innovation and design. They began in 1991, initially focusing on product design and engineering but soon realized their human-centred approach went beyond products and services to designing organizational change. IDEO partner Whitney Mortimer explains:

> We saw how far design could go to address new kinds of challenges facing business and society. The challenges were complex, they were human, and they were system-based. We were starting to understand how design could have broader impact and that we needed to rethink how we talked about design ... It was thought of as a form, objects, and beauty. It still may be all of those things, but we weren't focused on the noun anymore. We were focused on the verb, and we started talking about an approach and a mindset.[3]

In the context of this book, IDEO's partnership story with Cineplanet in Peru could be used as an exemplar of collaboration or creativity or critical reflection. In this chapter, we will discuss IDEO's work as an exemplar of communication, although it is evident IDEO's approach is truly collaborative, creative and critically reflective as well. In organizations that embed the 4Cs, all of them are frequently evident, co-existing and interacting all the time. Communication is paramount to IDEO, and it is apparent in Whitney Mortimer's reflections: 'we needed to rethink how we talked about design. . . . We were focused on the verb, and we started talking about an approach and a mindset.'[4] How we talk, the way we use language, how we communicate and how we understand communication has profound consequences for an organization's culture. In fact, communication fundamentally addresses how organizations actually organize themselves.[5]

IDEO's design thinking, innovation and organizational change work unfolds in what they describe as the 'context of a complicated, networked and messily human organization'.[6] To navigate these organizational dynamics requires a human-centred approach to communication. For IDEO, essential to that approach is the use of 'story' and 'empathy'. IDEO partner Diego Rodriguez explains: 'In essence, what you do in the human-centred design process is go out into the world to gain empathy for somebody else's existence. All of us have a different story, so it's really important to understand what's happening in someone's life and how your design solution might change it for the better.'[7] Communication and connection through story and empathy is not only IDEO's approach to design, it is an approach that influences the way they work within their own organization and how they engage with partners such as Cineplanet. In IDEO's approach, our coherence maker for understanding communication processes, the 'Communication Crystal' is evident.

The Cineplanet and IDEO collaboration began by engaging Cineplanet's Mildreth Maldonado as an embedded member of IDEO's design team. It started with a tour of Peru and Chile (where Cineplanet also has cinemas) visiting movie theatres, conducting interviews, observing how cinema goers interact with Cineplanet, and how people gather and socialize in Peru's parks, churches and other public spaces. IDEO refer to this as an 'exploratory phase'[8] and it is a process of seeking research and inspiration through observation and synthesis. This research and observation phase is *alert to messaging* in our Communication Crystal coherence maker. The deep noticing in IDEO's exploratory phase is communication that requires being hyper-aware and open to the situation and signals around you. In this first phase Maldonado, as an embedded client team member, describes her experience:

It worked out much better than I thought in the beginning because I had to learn the methodology, but we learned how to work together. That's why I feel very much a part of the team, and not just a client. I was the link that helped the team understand how the Peruvian market and the Peruvian customer work. It's not just about my knowledge of the industry, but also about being able to relate to our culture, our people, and to understand the customer.[9]

This experience reveals IDEO's human-centred approach to communication. It values and enables the stories of many voices – those of the customers, those of their client Cineplanet and those voices that represent the Peruvian cultural experience. In the coherence maker the Communication Crystal, this is *enabling voice*. Rather than traditional market research, IDEO's design team sought inspiration from in-context interviews (in cinema queues, DVD stores, people's homes) to generate stories and insights about users' desires and motivations.

The team also created impromptu drawings and ideas that responded to their emerging insights and gained immediate feedback from customers. In the Communication Crystal, the intent and effectiveness of communicating ideas is *conveying meaning and purpose*. For IDEO the purpose of these 'sacrificial concepts'[10] allows them to see how people perceive ideas in their early stages. The IDEO team is not beholden to these concepts and they are easily discarded, but they help in generating and refining ideas throughout the process. After the separate fieldwork observations, testimonies and insights, the design team shared their experiences with each other as storytelling sessions. From the stories and raw data, themes and possibilities began to emerge and come together.

In IDEO's design approach is a communication process that allows ideas to be generated from close observation and many voices. These ideas are then developed and refined by further action, and in the Communication Crystal this is *generating action and agency*. In this early phase of the design process, it is evident that the type of communication IDEO is using is sensitive to the authentic experience they are seeking to comprehend. Fundamental to IDEO's design practice is communication that is interactive, narrative based and empowering. Communication for IDEO is more than a one-way transmission; it is about making sense of human experience through empathy with people and the world around them by sharing, constructing and synthesing stories. Media theorist Marshall McLuhan famously said, 'the medium is the message'[11] and this explains how an organization (as the medium) is how it communicates (the message). The way an organization like IDEO communicates is what the organization is. This is a concept that is sometimes difficult for organizations to comprehend, since communication, organization and knowledge are treated as separate entities. Our definition of communication brings these concepts together.

Defining communication

When humans communicate we express what we know and we make meaning, and every time we do that, we shape who we think we are. This applies as much to individuals as it does to organizations. Through communicating we continue to construct, co-construct and re-construct our reality, combining the psychology of our internal structures with the external structures of our environment. We are in essence, as individuals or organizations, how and what we communicate, and all organizational knowledge and operational processes can only exist by being expressed as communication. Communication expert Milton N. Campos' definition of communication describes the dual ecosystem for communication in this way:

> Communication should be understood as a transversal discipline that crosses all others because it is both psychological and social and because it accounts for necessary and particular contingent knowledge. Communication is the foundation of all scientific disciplines and all forms of human expression (eg. art, common sense codes) because it is simultaneously a condition and result of all possible human knowledge.[12]

Communication is fundamental to both understanding and creating knowledge, and sets the agenda for what we know and how we see ourselves. This is illustrated by the comment of former US Federal Reserve (the Fed) Chairman, Ben Bernanke when he said, 'monetary policy is 98% talk and 2% action'.[13] Bernanke's message here is that communication *is* knowledge, and his aim as the chairman was to make the Fed more transparent by communicating and explaining its policies more regularly at press conferences, and in other media. This is how communication sets the agenda of what we know, or as communication researcher John T Warren argued: 'Each utterance makes the world; other choices make different worlds.'[14]

This is why the communication of untruths is powerful and concerning in creating a new reality (or different worlds). As novelist Salmon Rushdie in 2017 noted: 'The White House, from which all untrue flows, is now flipping it and accusing its opponents in the mainstream media of being liars. It's very worrying because if we are going to live in a country in which truth is an aspect of your belief system, then that's a very unstable society.'[15] We then have to define communication as *true* communication based not on belief systems but on integrity, accountability and humility. True communication has to be imbued with critical reflection and genuine collaboration, as educator and philosopher Paulo Freire points out:

> The naming of the world, through which people constantly re-create that world, cannot be an act of arrogance. Dialogue, as the encounter of those addressed to the common task of learning and acting, is broken if the parties (or one of them) lack humility. How can I dialogue if I always project ignorance onto others and never perceive my own? ... How can I dialogue if I am closed to – and even offended by – the contribution of others?[16]

The key to true communication is a self-perception of our own ignorance and openness to the contribution of others and this requires empathy, risktaking and commitment. We conceive communication as an ethical, mutually empowering and empathic dialogue (with agreement and contestation) based on truth, where, to quote author George Orwell in *1984*, there is 'the freedom to say that two plus two make four'.[17] Generating agency and empowerment through communication is central to our understanding of communication and how organizations can organize and transform through the 4Cs. In this chapter we explain the ethics and empowerment of organizational communication through the coherence maker, the Communication Crystal. Before we do, we need to understand why communication is so often misunderstood.

Myth-busting ideas about communication

Misconceptions have arisen about communication from a number of assumptions that continue to be perpetuated in organizations. We need to debunk these assumptions to understand what true communication really is. This leads us to busting the first myth that communication is considered only one aspect of an organization, when in reality communication is the threads of the fabric that actually make an organization. One of the great assumptions about organizational communication is that it sits only with Human Relations, Public Relations, 'spin doctors' or the Communication Team. In reality, communication is present in everything an organization does and comes to define an organization.

Myth 1: Communication is only one aspect of an organization, such as public relations

Communication has to be considered more than the image, branding and rhetoric of an organization. Authentic communication is about the organization's reality. At IDEO, the reality of being a human-centred and innovative workplace is the way colleagues work and communicate with each other, and with their collaborative partners. Open and authentic communication is present in all aspects of the organization's culture and climate. A description of the workplace illustrates how the way IDEO communicates pervades every aspect of the organization:

> IDEO had a very flat organizational structure. The desks of partners and senior leaders were interspersed among those of junior designers, which promoted a spirit of openness and accessibility. The layout of IDEO spaces engendered interaction ... Employees were encouraged to express themselves, which extended to the design and personalization of their work environments. Walking through an IDEO office, one might encounter a seven-foot-tall sea monster costume, an oversized origami sculpture, a Nordic fish lamp, or collections of past products and design prototypes. Posters of IDEO's core values and sticky notes from brainstorming sessions covered the walls.[18]

The working environment of IDEO is not a stylist's fabrication; it is the reality of the type of communication the organization tacitly and explicitly values. It is a reality that IDEO wants their employees to have a 'voice' in. In this instance, the rhetoric of communication texts such as the '*Little Book of IDEO*'[19] is the reality of the open-ended, interactive communication within the organization. The type of communication valued at IDEO is essential and fundamental to its core values, which are:[20]

1 Be Optimistic,

2 Collaborate,

3 Take ownership,

4 Embrace ambiguity,

5 Talk less, do more,

6   Learn from failure,

7   Make others successful.

The nature of communication in an organization represents what knowledge is valued, and how power is exercised. Alternatively, how power and control is exercised in an organization is normalized and ingrained through communication. Power or powerlessness is embedded in the everyday talk and all aspects of organizational communication (meetings, emails, blogs, newsletters, websites etc.). We argue that to be 'true' communication it must be related to the power of agency and self-efficacy. Communication that creates agency is complex and goes beyond the myth that communication is one-way, or even two-way.

Myth 2: Communication is one-way

The myth that communication is one-way has been perpetuated by the command-and-control approach to management. Organizational communication that developed in the early twentieth century was based on an engineering perspective and saw communication as a downward, one-way transmission of information for employees to understand and follow orders. Communication in this organizational structure is a top-down, management controlled activity (the VW case study in Chapter 6 provides a stark example of this approach). The legacy of this straightforward but disempowering approach to communication is still obvious and widespread today.[21]

We argue that the power of communication is in it being interactive and polyphonic (many perspectives and voices). More recent organizational communication theory[22] emphasizes the importance of participation by multiple stakeholders to deal with the complexity of organizational environments. The more interactive the communication is in an organization, the more the individual has a part in transforming an organization.

Communication is the interactive prism (or crystal) through which the individual and the organization as a social group construct and re-construct their reality. An organization such as IDEO embraces communication that is interactive and polyphonic, and so it becomes their organizational reality.

After the 'exploratory phase' for example, IDEO's 'concepting phase' involves developing ideas through an iterative process of moving between frameworks and brainstorming, and their polyphonic approach to communication through multiple angles is evident in their collaboration with Cineplanet: 'Team members discussed emerging concepts vigorously. During this process, designers would often reflect on user stories, frameworks, and behaviours to assess the alignment of potential solutions with the insights that surfaced in the previous phase. Simultaneously, the business implications of concepts and the technical considerations of their implementation were explored to ensure efficacy from multiple angles.'[23] IDEO's brainstorming rules also illustrate the polyphonic and interactive communication they value. The rules are:

1   Defer judgement.

2   Encourage wild ideas.

3   Build on the ideas of others.

4   Stay focused on the topic.

5   One conversation at a time.

6   Be visual.

7   Go for quantity.[24]

Polyphonic rather than one-way communication is also associated with self-organizing complexity and generating creativity in organizations. Direct one-way communication intervention can undermine the self-organizing, generative potential of a complex system. Researcher Chris Bilton argues: 'One important priority for managers, especially in their communication strategies, is to ensure that communication does not become too overly strategic; scope is needed for the unexpected connections and multiple networks layering outwards from the immediate organizational priorities.'[25] Controlling communication in an organization is detrimental to allowing a polyphonic and complex system to bloom. Communication also needs to be understood as multimodal, and this deals with the next myth.

Myth 3: Communication is only spoken and written language

This myth is debunked in IDEO's brainstorming rules when it says, 'Be visual'. Communication is the way we express and make meaning, and so our thinking and feeling is shaped by the way we communicate.[26] If communication is limited only to the spoken and the written word, the potential to open up thinking through other expressive modes such as images is diminished. Visual representations such as sketches, diagrams, maps and visual metaphors are not just another form of expression, they are another way of generating thinking. Communication and hence ideas can be activated and expressed by all the senses – by seeing, hearing, feeling, smelling and moving the body. Approaching communication in a 'multimodal' way is to explore the visual, the sensory and the embodied to access and develop different ways of thinking beyond speaking and writing[27] (see reference to performance artist Marina Abramović's work in Chapter 5 as an example of a visual, sensory and embodied experience that generates many ideas). The immersive experience IDEO had in the exploratory phase in Peru was an embodied cultural perspective that involved developing understanding and ideas activated by all the senses (not just seeing, but hearing, feeling and smelling). Recognizing and exploring different communication modes, such as sensory and embodied modes, can reveal many fresh and diverse ideas and perspectives.

In communication, semiotics is the study of how meaning is expressed through multiple sign systems or codes such as words, images, videos, numbers, formulaes, songs, gestures, dance etc. Combining different multidisciplinary communication systems is described as *bricolage* and *intertextuality* in semiotics. Bricolage and intertextuality refer to the construction of new meanings made from the connections of multiple signs with past meanings.[28] IDEO illustrates how ideas are developed through an interdisciplinary and multimodal approach in their 'prototyping phase':

> Throughout this process, designers and client employees outside of the project's team who were assisting with the field text would constantly communicate in order to bring as many perspectives as possible to bear on the performance of the prototypes. For example, a designer with a background in business operations might have ideas on how to improve a prototype's efficiency. Another designer with a degree in behavioural psychology might see the patterns in how a prototype affected group dynamics. A client employee who was familiar with the normal behaviour of a business's customers might be well placed to predict and note how a prototype might integrate with the existing operation.[29]

Multimodal communication and an interdisciplinary approach opens up multiple possibilities and perspectives in an organization's capacity to develop thinking and learning. The quality of the spoken and written word, however, is still central and highly significant in human relationships and affects the way we use technology to communicate in organizations.

Myth 4: Technology solves all communication problems

Technology is a great enabler of communication for the spoken and written word, and other multimodal forms such as images, videos and podcasts. The increasing sophistication of technology improves access to communication (video conferencing that instructs surgery in remote communities for example, and artificial intelligence that is able to answer and fix technology breakdowns) but human qualities in communication shape the quality and ethical use of technology. It is the interpersonal quality of relating to others and relating ideas to others that by extension affects the quality of communication with technology. How we think and reason through empathy, influence and collaborating impacts the quality and nature of communication with technology.[30] The primacy of human qualities solves communication problems.

The intimacy and inclusion in IDEO's human-to-human communication influences their digital communication presence.[31] In both their human-to-human communication, and communication through technology, there is a human-centredness that facilitates human agency. As we move increasingly to a world of artificial intelligence, organizations will have to consider and respond to the agency not only of humans but also of machines as well.[32] How communication can structure and power human (and possibly non-human) agency in an organization is woven into the integral relationship communication has with the other Cs.

Communication and the other Cs

Without the agency of communication, the other Cs cannot be given impetus and action. The relationship between communication and creativity, critical reflection and collaboration is symbiotic but also complex. We explore that relationship through the synthesis and wisdom of paradoxes. To begin, creativity needs uncertainty to allow for the freedom to experiment, but it also needs the certainty of communication to ultimately 'sell' creative ideas.

Communication and creativity: the paradox of certainty and uncertainty

IDEO embraces uncertainty in the creative process, for they believe, 'You have to be comfortable with starting with a blank sheet of paper – even relish it. You will have moments of doubt where you're not sure what to do.'[33] By playing with possibility (and the other iterative aspects of the Creativity Cascade – see Chapter 4) creative ideas come in bits and pieces and develop over time. Creativity is to tolerate uncertainty until you get the right idea. However, in the end, as creativity researcher Robert J. Sternberg argues, creative ideas do not sell themselves, they have to be sold with certainty and persuasion.[34] Creative ideas disturb the status quo and they are usually viewed with suspicion and misunderstanding, so communication is used to persuade people of the certainty of the right idea. According to Sternberg, 'From the investment view, then, the creative person buys low by presenting an idea that initially is not valued and then attempting to convince others of its value.'[35] The uncertainty of creativity needs the certainty of persuasive communication. The type of persuasive communication that sells ideas is shaped by communication's paradoxical relationship with critical reflection.

Communication and critical reflection: the paradox of persuasion and integrity

Persuasive communication is often perceived as the 'hard sell' of making a case and driving the point home. Given that we argue communication is more than one way (it is polyphonic) and should generate agency, our understanding of persuasive communication is informed by critical reflection. Certainly, communication can be manipulative and deceptive, but in the 4Cs approach it is not about moving people to a new position by threatening, guilting, begging or cajoling, it is persuading through credibility and integrity, by being honest and critically reflective. Paradoxically persuasion is more effective in changing people's ideas when it is a negotiated, co-constructed process. Leadership expert Jay Conger argues, persuasion is:

> a process of learning from others and negotiating a shared solution. To that end, persuasion consists of these essential elements: establishing credibility, framing to find the common ground, providing vivid evidence, and connecting emotionally. Credibility grows … out of two sources: expertise and relationships. The former is a function of product or process knowledge and the latter a history of listening to and working in the best interest of others.[36]

Critical reflection encourages the most effective persuaders not to be closed-minded or dogmatic but able to question and get others to question their own assumptions (see the Critical Reflection Crucible in Chapter 5). Generating integrity and agency through communication depends upon both critical reflection and collaboration.

Communication and collaboration: the paradox of convergence and divergence

Collaboration is about exploring the richness of divergent ideas from multiple perspectives and stakeholders (see Collaboration Circles in Chapter 7). To cross-pollinate perspectives and collaborate on design projects, IDEO for instance employs people with diverse backgrounds in psychology, business, linguistics, art and architecture. With collaboration comes divergence, but divergence ultimately has to be communicated clearly as a synthesized, convergent idea. From the divergence of many ideas, a convergent idea or shared vision must have the capacity to be communicated. The clarity of meaning and purpose in effective communication allows the divergence of different perspectives in collaboration to come together. Clarity of meaning and purpose, and convergence in understanding is what we also achieve through the coherence maker, the Communication Crystal (Figure 7.2).

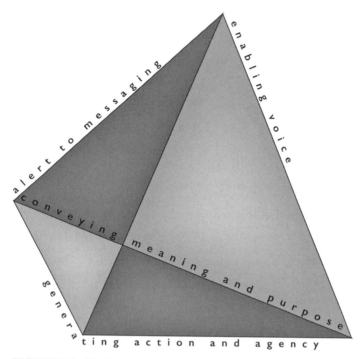

FIGURE 7.2 *The Communication Crystal.*

A process for communication: the Communication Crystal

We have used the metaphor of the crystal to suggest that communication is an interactive prism through which meaning is made between the individual in an organization and the social group that is the organization. A crystal with its many surfaces also means communication is multimodal and polyphonic and can be sent and received in multiple ways. Although organizations are complex, the ordered patterns of a crystal suggest communication brings structure and clarity to the way an organization understands and projects itself. Communication is bound up with identity, for through it an organization constantly re-constructs its own reality. Perception and identity are manifest by communication and relationships deep within an organization.[37] Although communication is ubiquitous in organizations, it is not necessarily deeply understood and its potential for 4C transformation not realized. Our coherence maker, the Communication Crystal, is a tangible way to explore the transforming potential of communication, and has the following stages:

- ◢ Alert to messaging.

- ◢ Enabling voice.

- ◢ Conveying meaning and purpose.

- ◢ Generating action and agency.

Communication in whatever mode or representation (through the body, voice, visual, aural, tactile, sensory, or mediated with technology) must firstly be *noticed* or perceived. Noticing messaging is not just *what* is being represented but *how* it is being represented. The Communication Crystal coherence maker begins an understanding of communication by noticing and being *alert to messaging*.

Alert to messaging

Rather than simply being aware of sending or receiving a message, 'alert to messaging' is a heightened, reflexive two-way state. Reflexivity is to see ourselves critically; it is to be accountable for what we say and how we say it. 'Alert to messaging' is to consider how what we say affects others and how we receive messages affects others. This alertness is an active and energized state of meta-awareness, and it is learnt through mindfulness, responsibility and practice.

The hyper-awareness of messaging begins with people noticing the verbal and non-verbal dimensions of oral language. Being alert to the non-verbal or paralinguistic aspects of communication is to listen attentively and notice and interpret vocal expression, gestures and body language, proximity between people, energy and silences. Developing an 'alertness to messaging' is in realizing for example:

- bodies facing each other improves group communication;

- eyes and attentive listening to someone speaking improves the communicators messaging;

- probing questions and empathy towards the speaker improves listening;

- sitting in a circle creates a sense of community and equality;

- controlling the paralanguage of gesture and body language improves the effectiveness of speaking;

- there are ways in which everyone can be given opportunity and responsibility to communicate.[38]

Being alert to messaging strengthens an awareness of how communication is linked to the way we organize and build knowledge in organizations. For instance, a complex state of communication in an organization generates collaboration, creativity and innovation. A complex state of communication operates at the boundary of order and chaos, between organized structures and the chaos of incoherence. Creativity resides on the edge of this boundary; this is where the emergence of new ideas occur. To develop complex communication in an organization, collaborators must be alert to the frequency, procedures, roles and assumptions of the messaging in a group.[39] Academic Abran J. Salazar describes evidence of complex communications:

Whenever we see group members changing their interaction patterns, whether by changing the frequency and directional flow of communication, using new procedures to solve problems or make decisions, displaying little or no discussion typical of group member roles, or questioning or supplanting assumptions about what counts as good or bad information, the group is showing evidence of operating in a complex state.[40]

Organizational members aware of and practiced in complex communication processes are more able to collaborate, reflect critically and generate creativity and innovation. In the 4Cs approach we encourage communication processes that develop 'noticings' in and 'disruption' (similar to the small data approach mentioned in Chapter 5) to the routine rituals of communication. To be alert to or meta-aware of the noticings and disruptors that engender a complex state of communication the following questions need to be considered:

- How often has each group member spoken?
- How are new ways being used to look at ideas and issues?
- How are group members' roles shaping a typical flow and outcome in the discussion?
- What assumptions are continually being made?

Complex processes in communication can only be developed if organization members and leaders have a reflexive awareness of noticing these processes. Complexity and reflexivity in communication are apparent in IDEO's brainstorming rules: defer judgement, encourage wild ideas, build on others' ideas, go for quantity. When communication processes are noticed, *enabling all voices* is the next step in developing communication.

Enabling voice

Enabling voice is creating the positive conditions that allow all individuals to express their thinking, and to be open to receive others' thinking. In our definition, communication is the expression of the individual's voice through any form of messaging. We recognize the primacy of speaking and embodiment but other forms of communication – writing, reading, numeracy and representations that are visual, spatial and bodily, or mediated through instruments and technology – are also an expression of human voice and organizational reality. In the 4Cs approach all voices must be heard, supported and challenged through expression in a range of communication modes.

Individual agency and the 'genius' of the group can only be realized when all voices are enabled. To enable all voices, no one voice can dominate. Through implemented communication strategies, dominant voices can learn to generously let others communicate, and unconfident or unpractised communicators given support and space to find their voices. There are environmental, individual and group dynamic factors that can hinder the enabling of the voice in organizations. In group communication the following factors[41] have to be addressed with communication strategies to enable all voices:

1   Time pressures (make time for voices to be confident and expressed).

2   Organizational culture (allow risk taking in thinking).

3   Functional fixedness (break habits of thinking).

4   Evaluation apprehension (break fear of being judged).

5   Production blocking (find ways for expression of all voices).

6   Network structures (break ritualised patterns in communication).

Time pressures inhibit communication, as there is not enough space for group members to adequately express their thoughts. In group communication, time has to be devoted to enable group members to express their thinking, and to implement strategies that develop the members' abilities to put thinking into words or representations. This may include strategies such as sharing in a pair or group first, brainstorming with post-it notes, being visual by drawing or embodying an idea as a 'tableau' (frozen 3D human picture), and then sharing or exhibiting ideas back to the larger group ('jigsawing') for feedback. Time in organizational learning has to be spent developing confidence in effective communication skills that are authentic and interactive.

Another factor that affects communication is the patterns and structures of an *organizational culture* that prevent risk taking in thinking. Being risk averse in an organization may be indicated by members only willing to express a 'right' answer, or reluctant to creatively problem solve. A risk taking culture values divergent and challenging thinking and openly and continually acknowledges learning from mistakes. To take risks in thinking is to let go of self-censorship and the fear of making a mistake. Communicating thinking in the public sphere is taking a risk and an organizational environment has to model and support this leap of faith for its members.

Enabling the voice can also be constrained by factors related to individual *functional fixedness* and *evaluation apprehension*. Functional fixedness refers to a person's habitual ways of thinking in a situation. Varying communication strategies, such as drawing an abstract picture to explain your thinking, creating an embodied 'postcard' or brainstorming salient words, can be used to explore different ways of enabling voice, and developing flexible and divergent thinking in organizational contexts. Evaluation apprehension is when people refrain from expressing their thoughts for fear of being judged or seen in a negative light. Voices can only be enabled and valued in a positive culture and it is through modelling, learning and feedback that open communication skills are valued and affirmed.

To enable individual voices the dynamic of group communication is navigated in terms of *production blocking* and *network structures*. Production blocking is when people are inhibited from communicating because someone else is already communicating. Put simply, we can not talk at the same time and we have to wait for our turn. This can lead to production blocking because not everyone may be able to contribute at the right time. Network structure is the patterning of communication among people, for instance one person in a group may always lead discussions, another may always have the final word, or another will usually wait to be asked to contribute. These characteristics can be mindfully addressed by varying the configurations, opportunities and types of communication. For example, working individually online for a group brainstorm or discussion, or groups communicating non-verbally by constructing images or a tableau, or small groups discussing ideas and 'jigsawing' those ideas back to a larger group. All of these strategies enable voices by varying the production and structures of communication.

To enable all voices takes time, practice and feedback, but the 'fruit' of these labours is the development of complex communication skills to collaborate, reflect and create. Communication can be any form appropriation for knowledge creation and audience. Whether it is a speech, discussion, inquiry, experiment, poem, report, dance, diagram, formula or code, it needs to be framed and understood as a means of communication and enablement of a person's thinking, or the group's or organization's thinking. Being alert to messaging is awareness of communication and enabling voice provides the opportunity to communicate. Awareness and enablement allow communicators to begin to construct and co-construct meaning. These first two aspects of the Communication Crystal are only effective if the *meaning* of the message is *conveyed* with *purpose* and control.

Conveying meaning and purpose

When a message is conveyed there has to be shared understanding between the communicator and their audience. Unless communication is considered an interactive process, its purpose is unclear and meaning is not exchanged or integrated. It is not enough to have an opportunity to voice and communicate; it requires a crafting of skills to share meaning with others. To convey meaning and purpose requires both the communicator and the audience to be skilled and conversant in the form of communication being used.

The type of communication chosen has to be conveyed and focused by a clear intentionality and purpose. For instance, an effective meeting can be alert to the messaging and enabling the voices of all participants, but what is said must also be meaningful to the meeting's purpose. Conveying meaning is achieved by controlling a particular communication medium for a specific intent and purpose. Other examples of conveying meaning and purpose in a medium can be in using vocal tone and non-verbal cues in a conversation, or crafting a persuasive argument in writing or capturing a mood in a photograph, or achieving clarity in a report. When communicating with technologies it may be manipulating a narrative through images and editing in video, or controlling the dynamic of rhythm and tone in electronic music, or using the appropriate font for a business logo. Conveying meaning and purpose in any form of communication are learnt skills in controlling the effectiveness, aesthetic and impact of different communication modes.

In the prototyping phase, IDEO had to convey their designs as tangible artefacts and processes to get feedback, and to test and refine their designs often as real-time observations with the client and customers. Without conveying precision in the meaning and intent of their designs they would not be able to communicate and get feedback from different perspectives. The clarity and aesthetic control of the design messages and mediums in which they were working meant other designers with different backgrounds could improve the prototype in diverse ways. To take on feedback, and make observations of customer interactions with the prototypes, takes the IDEO designers back to being *alert to messaging* and *enabling voice*. As with all our coherence makers, the Communication Crystal is iterative and recursive in its processes. By manipulating the medium and aesthetics of communication, organizations can control the meaning and purpose of messaging to then *generate action and agency* as the last step in the Communication Crystal.

Generating action and agency

Communication in our view is a dynamic process that produces action and agency, rather than disempowerment and compliance. Communication in an Orwellian totalitarian state is a broadcast to maintain social and individual control through constraint and suppression. In the 4C approach, communication is a social interaction that actively creates meaningful relationships, social activity and empowerment.[42] Communication is more than reflecting or representing an idea, it is an interactive phenomenon that is fundamentally humanising and enables thought, reason and identity creation.[43] True human-centred communication generates action and agency.

Action and agency is evident in the objectives of IDEO's core values: be optimistic, take ownership, talk less, do more and make others successful. Their aim to generate action and agency through their design thinking and communication was captured when IDEO partner Diego Rodriguez said, 'All of us have a different story, so it's really important to understand what's happening in someone's life and how your design solution might change it for the better.'[44] Their client partner Cineplanet anticipated the agency they would gain from their IDEO partnership; they saw it was the beginning of not just new ideas but a deep organizational and cultural change. The action and agency generated by communication would involve shifting the company from one that excelled in business operations to one that focused more on customer needs and desires, and in doing so transform the dynamic and culture of Cineplanet.

Paulo Freire[45] argues that communication profoundly underpins an individual's empowerment and existential sense of being. Communication is a potentially transformational and humanising force, it must be treated as a dialogue of engagement and participation, and an ethical act of co-constructed creation between people. If communication is not mediated by trust, humility and critical reflection, the human voice and identity are suppressed, and the organizational culture will not be defined by empowered individuals. Too often, people are ignored, dealt with abruptly, not given responsibility and told what to do. All these actions undermine trust and faith in others, and represent a lack of true communication.

Praxis is a term to describe how practice, dialogue and reflection can work together to inform and generate our actions. In the spirit of praxis, communication generates action and agency only when infused with critical reflection and collaborative practice. Communication as action and agency should not be a form of domination and oppression, but through praxis, a thoughtful means to meet the world and challenge it.[46] Action and agency is to engage with the world critically and compassionately, and to see others and ourselves as complex beings striving for meaning and purpose. Communication is a conduit for generating individual action and agency but it needs to be framed wisely, ethically and morally. How we communicate depends on ethical choices. According to Milton N. Campos[47] communication *is* ethics as it constructs and shapes how we love, understand, co-operate, hate, war and destroy. Communication has to be conceived of as a dialogue that can construct and destroy power relations and generate new ways of thinking, being and relating to others. It is through this type of communication that organizations can take social action and transform.

Learning skills and understandings in communication have been found to: enhance organizational processes and organizational life; address concerns in the twenty-first century; help to improve the educational enterprise; develop the whole person; encourage being a responsible participant in the world, socially and culturally; and help individuals succeed in their careers and in business.[48] These ideas indicate how communication is an essential competency for organizations to respond to the challenges of the twenty-first century.

Communication starts with:

- *Alert to messaging* – being hyper-aware of affecting others by what we say, how we say it and how we receive messages.

- *Enabling voice* – creating opportunities and capacities for all voices to be expressed.

- *Conveying meaning and purpose* – crafting skills in communication so that messages have clarity as shared interpretation and intent between people.

- *Generating action and agency* – interacting through communication as a dynamic to empower the efficacy of relationships, knowledge and activity.

Getting started: building communication in organizations

Building true communication requires an organization to ask the following big questions.

How is 4C communication in your organization:

1   Active and agentic

    How does the organizations communication generate action and agency?

2   Central

    How can 4C communication be at the core of the organization's reality?

3   Multimodal

    What types of multimodal communication are used for idea generation in the organization?

4   Connected

    How is communication linked to creativity, critical reflection and collaboration in the organization?

5   Applied

    Where and when can the Communication Crystal coherence maker be implemented and sustained to generate action and agency?

The next chapter explores how collaboration nurtures communication, creativity and critical reflection in an organization.

8

Collaboration

A community health worker case manager visited a patient's home in a public housing development in East Baltimore, Maryland, four times before being able to make contact with the patient. The patient needed thyroid surgery but would not continue with her medical care as she had a deep fear and distrust of male doctors and the medical facility where she received her care. The visiting health worker was from a grassroots, community-based organization called 'Sisters Together and Reaching'. This organization was a partner in the new Johns Hopkins Community Health Partnership which was delivering

FIGURE 8.1 *Collaboration can break down silos of knowledge and expertise.*

an innovative model in collaborative patient-centred care through multidisciplinary teams. The story of the visiting community health worker and the East Balimore patient[1] will begin this chapter to explain how collaboration and transformation can break down 'silos' of delivery and knowledge to deal with complex issues. We will also illustrate how stages in our Collaboration Circles coherence maker are evident in the story.

A case study in collaboration: the Johns Hopkins Community Health Partnership[2]

When visiting the patient's home, the community health worker observed that there were several electrical cords running through the house, leading out of the window. She explained to the patient it was a fire hazard to have so many extension cords connected to a single socket inside her home. It transpired that only one of the electrical sockets in the patient's home was working and her neighbour had allowed her to run an extension cord into her home to keep her refrigerator and stove operating. The health worker asked if the patient could co-construct with her a 'barriers to care assessment', and the patient agreed.

In our coherence maker, this agreement to collaborate and construct a shared endeavour begins with the process of *offering* and *yielding*. In the 'barriers to care assessment' the patient and health worker both reviewed the patient's goals and objectives – one of which was resolving the electrical issues. The health worker was able to arrange an appointment with the Housing Authority within two weeks to not only address this issue, but to deal with other issues in the home. The health worker was able to re-assign the patient to a female medical provider and to schedule her needed thyroid surgery.

Reviewing the 'barriers to care assessment' with the patient, and the steps taken from that moment on, resulted from collaboration with the patient, and the partnered health and social care providers in the Johns Hopkins Community Health Partnership (J-CHiP). These steps involved dealing with and resolving all the interconnected issues that had previously prevented the patient from achieving medical care. Before J-CHiP, the issues the patient faced were disconnected by health and social care services separated and siloed from one another. In our coherence maker, the collaborative process of rigorously addressing and developing the interconnected issues is *challenging, evaluating and extending*. The ultimate aim of a collaboration is a combined construction of ideas and actions that generates on-going connections. In our Collaboration Circles coherence maker this is *advancing co-constructions and connections*. In the story of the East Baltimore patient, once her healthcare, housing, and other social determinants of health were addressed, she had more time to focus on other goals in her life, and the patient has since graduated from school as a Certified Medical Assistant.

This story is an example of how the Johns Hopkins Community Health Partnership initiative (J-CHiP) transformed healthcare delivery and outcomes through collaborative practice. Collaboration in this example happened on a number of levels, between:

- the patient and the community health worker;
- the community health worker and the medical health providers; and
- community organizations, the health providers and the social needs of the community.

In this chapter the Johns Hopkins Community Health Partnership case study will demonstrate not only the powerful benefits but also the challenges of collaboration. It reveals how structures in organizations must be developed for collaboration, and how there are processes to truly collaborate. This health sector partnership highlights how collaborative processes can become the engine that drives innovation and transformation. How then did the Johns

Hopkins Community Health Partnership 'catalyze true delivery transformation through genuine collaboration'?[3]

Johns Hopkins Medicine (JHM) is an integrated health enterprise between Johns Hopkins University School and the Johns Hopkins Health System (which includes the Johns Hopkins Hospital). JHM had a historically strained relationship with the inner city residents of East Baltimore and for decades these 200,000 residents experienced an ambivalent and often troubled relationship with the Johns Hopkins Health System. The East Baltimore community has significant social, chronic illness and economic challenges, and a life expectancy up to twenty years less than in nearby more affluent Baltimore communities. JHM recognized they had a poor relationship with this urban community and realized the health sector's culture of siloing services needed to change to better meet the complex health and social needs of East Baltimore residents. JHM realized they needed to innovate in healthcare delivery with this community and so developed the Johns Hopkins Community Health Partnership (J-CHiP), a new patient-centred care programme that created a collaboration of services in patients' homes, community clinics, acute care hospitals, emergency departments, and skilled nursing facilities.

JHM realized they could only improve outcomes if clinical care and the social determinants of health (such as housing, work, unemployment, food, social support, early life, transportation, addiction etc.) were addressed together. The partnership combined community-based and multi-disciplinary care intervention with the patients' primary care provider. Integrating healthcare delivery in this way was a radical departure from the traditional, siloed 'business as usual approach' to healthcare.

The Johns Hopkins Community Health Partnership was not, however, just an integration of complex health and social services, it also meant achieving better patient and broader community engagement by understanding the local context, the neighbourhood needs and establishing true partnerships and trust with the community. This was done in a number of ways and began by involving two grassroots community-based non-profit organizations who had worked long-term with the community; the Sisters Together and Reaching, and the Men and Families Center.

The Sisters Together and Reaching is a non-profit organization with twenty-five years' experience in providing direct case management, community health education and support services with HIV impacted communities and low-income minority communities struggling with chronic illness. This organization seeks to empower communities to make healthy lifestyle choices. The Men and Families Center is a non-profit community centre with more than seventeen years' experience providing support services such as parenting and life skills, finding employment and housing, and accessing clinical services. Engagement with partnerships like these was more than integrating social and health services; it was also the beginning of building stronger and engaged relationships with the community.

The main aim of the Johns Hopkins Community Health Partnership was to broaden community involvement and develop an inclusive, team-based approach that ultimately promoted patient engagement and more sustainable health and social outcomes. Care delivery was transformed through true collaboration with patients, their communities and health services. J-CHiP facilitated structures for collaboration and integration, but they also realized collaboration is a human process facilitated by particular relationships, dialogues and actions. Collaboration is not simply a matter of bringing people together and working together. So, what then is collaboration?

Defining true collaboration

True collaboration is not people co-operating, sharing ideas and working together. We argue collaboration is the beneficial mutuality of a shared vision, and the engine for agency, creativity, emergence and innovation. If collaboration is explained as an 'affair of the mind',[4] then 'being a team player' or 'being co-operative' does not define collaboration. Collaboration as an 'affair of the mind' suggests it is an intense synergy of ideas, goals, trust and relationships between people. Collaboration leads to the co-construction of something that evolves from the interdependence and mutuality of everyone's influence. Everyone in a collaborative process has a role to play, and in that role must feel equal and empowered to realize a shared and co-constructed vision. The principle of collaboration is beneficial mutuality that expands beyond the self or single entity.

A premise of the 4Cs approach to organizational transformation is that through collaboration humans become their 'fuller selves', and organizations achieve their 'fuller potential'. It was through the mutuality of true collaboration and partnerships that Johns Hopkins Medicine as an organization expanded its potential. Patients as individuals were able to become their fuller selves in collaborating with the health system partners. Creativity scholar Vera John-Steiner argues, 'Through collaboration we can transcend the constraints of biology, of time, of habit, and achieve a fuller self, beyond the limitations and the talents of the isolated self.'[5]

To achieve the beneficial mutuality of collaboration, however, requires the navigation of complex dynamics in communication and relationships. This chapter is about those dynamics. It is about how the individual-self or individual-entity crucially develops, learns and actualizes their potential through the oscillations of collaboration. We have synthesised those processes and dynamics into a coherence maker: 'Collaboration Circles'. It is a supporting structure or scaffold to frame how collaboration can be understood, learnt and facilitated.

Collaboration is not new, it has been at the heart of human development from the meeting of minds in the agoras (meeting places) of Ancient Greece to online communities that we are more familiar with. As discussed in Chapter 5, the lone creative genius propelling human development is a myth. It is rather the genius of collaboration that allows for personal growth and human civilizations to flourish. So, why is collaboration in organizations like Johns Hopkins Medicine so innovative? Why is collaboration not common practice? Why do more organizations not embrace collaboration? To address these questions, we need to consider some of the myths around collaboration to understand why it is misunderstood and why many organizations find collaboration challenging and counter-cultural to the established ways of operating.

Myth-busting ideas about collaboration

Certain mythologies and assumptions have misinterpreted what collaboration really is. The first myth is that the work in 'collaboration' is never really shared, and that someone or some group ends up doing all the work.

Myth 1: One person (or group) ends up doing all the work

This myth is a throwaway comment that reveals a lack of understanding and skills in how to collaborate. Collaboration is a learnt process, and when it is not understood, learnt or practised, it fragments and does not create a whole. When 'teamwork' is in pieces, typically one person tries to pick them all up to try to make a whole. Hence the comment, 'one person ends up doing all the work anyway'.

Groups and partnerships who struggle with collaboration exhibit the following characteristics, according to organizational psychologist Paul Paulus:[6]

1   Social anxiety (individuals too afraid to put ideas out to the group).
2   Social loafing/free riders (lazy individuals that allow others to do the work).

3   An illusion of productivity (individuals who think they are working
    but are not being productive towards the group's objective).

4   Blocking (individuals who have all the 'best ideas' and block everyone
    else's).

5   Task-irrelevant behaviours (individuals off-task, unable to focus on the
    group's objective).

6   Cognitive load issues (individuals not coping with all the work
    required in the group's collaborative objective).

These groups suffer from social inhibitions (difficulties effectively
communicating with others) and cognitive interference (difficulties focusing
on and managing what needs to be achieved). Individuals can learn how to
overcome these obstacles by learning *how* to collaborate.

Myth 2: Not everyone can collaborate

In Project Aristotle (so named as a tribute to Aristotle's quote, 'the whole is
greater than the sum of its parts'), Google spent two years studying 180 teams
to find an 'algorithm' for the perfect team. What they found is that there is no
formula for the perfect team. Their research found that 'what really mattered
less was about who was on the team, and more about how the team worked
together'.[7] In their organization, Google discovered successful collaborations
shared five dynamics:

1   Psychological safety: Team members feel safe to take risks and be
    vulnerable in front of each other.

2   Dependability: Team members get things done on time and meet
    Google's high bar for excellence.

3   Structure and clarity: Team members have clear roles, plans and goals.

4   Meaning: Work is personally important to team members.

5   Impact: Team members think their work matters and creates
    change.[8]

These dynamics for collaboration can be learnt, if structures, processes and
language for those processes are made explicit and practised. Everyone has the
capacity to reap the benefits of collaboration if they know how. Each individual
learns at different speeds but the innate capacity for collaboration is there to be
developed in everyone. It begins from learning to play with others as a child, to
learning from and with others as adults. Like play in childhood, collaboration
is an emotional and intellectual process for stretching our capacities.
Collaboration goes beyond the biological constraints of independent
individualism to develop and deepen our capacity through the psychology of
social interactions. Our limitations as individuals (or individual entities) are
overcome through collaboration by amplifying, enhancing, refining and
challenging our individual vision and purpose. In the Organizational
Effectiveness Wheel (see Chapter 3), collaboration is a capacity that facilitates
more effective learning. The better you collaborate, the better you learn. True
collaboration expands the learning boundaries of the individual self and the
learning boundaries of an organization's potential. Everyone can collaborate, it
is whether they know how, or whether they want to learn how to actualize their
potential through collaboration.

Myth 3: Collaboration takes up too much time

Collaboration takes time to set up and to learn, but the investment of time has
an enormous payoff, which is new ways of thinking about things
(conceptualizations) and new ways of doing things (process). Collaboration,
like the other Cs (creativity, critical reflection and communication) fall into the
productivity paradox or 'mouse wheel conundrum'. The productivity paradox is
that we do not have time to collaborate because we are 'too busy being productive'.
It is too difficult to get off the mouse wheel of pressing problems to engage in

collaboration. Yet making time for effective and purposeful collaboration increases productivity, innovation and transformation.[9] Reflection and collaboration is sometimes addressed in annual strategic thinking sessions but typically do not infiltrate the operational fabric of organizations. The everyday pressing issues continue to spin the busy 'mouse wheel' of doing the work.

There are always competing demands of time in organizations, but time is amorphous and only given shape by what is valued, prioritized and acted upon. For Johns Hopkins Medicine, healthcare delivery is busy and pressing, but they gave time, resources and learning to reflect and collaborate on seeking better and more sustainable outcomes for the East Baltimore community. JHM knew it would take a huge amount of effort and planning to achieve transformation in a delivery system that had historically not emphasized and developed cross-silo collaboration. They recognized that collaboration was a daunting task, for the J-CHiP enterprise was as much about cultural transformation as structural transformation. To meet their ambitious aims, the Johns Hopkins Community Health Partnership:

> sought to leverage existing efforts while building additional infrastructure to further connect collaborating entities and drive the type of cultural transformation that would be necessary for success. Each challenge required significant thought, delineation of choices/options, building teams of stakeholders not typically engaged in planning, determination of realistic timelines for implementation to be able to meet development and reporting requirements, and the ability to adapt to unanticipated logistical hurdles within these complex social and organizational dynamics.[10]

Collaboration is not a means in itself for greater productivity, sustainability or cultural transformation. Collaboration is only effective when the purpose of collaborating is clear and fit for purpose. It is through the clarity of purpose in the shared endeavour (described by Google as 'structure, meaning and impact') that collaboration can generate cultural transformation. There has to be precision in what the collaboration is co-constructing and why. For the Johns Hopkins Community Health Partnership it was to 'improve clinical care within and across settings, to address the non-clinical determinants of health, and to ultimately improve healthcare utilization and costs'.[11] True collaboration must be productive; if not it becomes another 'mouse wheel' of inefficiency, imprecision and stress.[12]

Structures, technology and physical space have roles in supporting the leveraging of productive collaboration. Digital collaborative partnerships between organizations can share and integrate big data to create new possibilities in accuracy, efficiency and expertise leading to innovation and growth.[13] Johns Hopkins Medicine are continuing to develop technology solutions that capture and evaluate data and processes to build sustainable long-term models of care. However, technology, structures and physical space are only enablers for collaboration, they in themselves do not create productive collaboration. As Google found, physically sitting team members together in an office is not significantly connected with team effectiveness, it is merely an enabler for collaboration. For structural, physical and digital enablers to have affect, it is still the human dynamic of collaborating that has to be understood and practised.

Myth 4: High consensus and co-operation is collaboration

The term 'true collaboration' or 'genuine collaboration' or 'productive collaboration' has already been mentioned in this chapter. In previous chapters we have referred to 'true communication' but not referred to 'true creativity' or 'true critical reflection'. Creativity and critical reflection (as discussed in Chapters 5 and 6) are often understood as concepts that are either difficult or out of reach. This presents problems for creativity and critical reflection as many people feel they are unknowable and intangible. The issue with collaboration and communication is that people think they understand these concepts, but do not really fully comprehend what they are. Hence we have to attribute 'true' to what they really are. For instance, collaboration is often confused with consensus and co-operation, which are valid capacities in certain settings, but they are not collaboration.

High consensus in an organization's work climate appears to suggest a collaborative culture, but high consensus can be a negative climate that mitigates collaboration. High consensus behaviours can mean ideas and decisions are always negotiated and compromised to 'steady the boat', rather than 'rock the boat'. High consensus creates a climate where ideas cannot be 'left of field'. For collaboration, high consensus is just as problematic as low trust. Low trust is indicative of a restrictive, critical and low-risk culture. The divergent viewpoints and unique 'wild' ideas essential for the rich possibilities of collaboration cannot flourish in such an environment. On the other hand, high levels of consensus suggest a harmonious and cohesive organizational climate, but they have also been found not to generate unique 'wild' ideas.[14] Such organizations foster group dynamics that primarily maintain group harmony but a consequence of this is to fall into the trap of premature consensus and self-censorship. Differences of opinion go unchallenged and the potential for critical reflection and generating new ideas is lost. A climate for collaboration is not served by cultures of low trust or high consensus, as both do not encourage honest, critical and original thinking. Google refers to this behavioural climate of high trust and risk-taking for collaboration as 'psychological safety'.

> Psychological safety refers to an individual's perception of the consequences of taking an interpersonal risk or a belief that a team is safe for risk taking in the face of being seen as ignorant, incompetent, negative, or disruptive. In a team with high psychological safety, teammates feel safe to take risks around their team members. They feel confident that no one on the team

will embarrass or punish anyone else for admitting a mistake, asking a question, or offering a new idea.[15]

Collaboration must have a climate of psychological safety to allow for the dynamics of perspective taking and challenge to realize the 'genius' of the many in a group or partnership. Consensus driven decision making does not promote that dynamic. Consensus, however, is vital for diplomacy, and at times for political survival. Although harmony and compromises are necessary in certain contexts, they are not the dynamic of collaboration.

Co-operation can be a part of collaboration, but of itself is not collaboration. Psychology and education scholars, Seana Moran and Vera John-Steiner[16] explain collaboration as the high point of a gradient that runs from social interaction, to co-operation, to working together, to collaboration:

Social interaction involves two or more people talking or in exchange, cooperation adds the constraint of shared purpose, and working together often provides coordination of effort. But collaboration involves the intricate blending of skills, temperaments, effort and sometimes personalities to realise a shared vision of something new and useful.[17]

Co-operation is to share and agree on being a part of a common purpose, but collaboration requires an interdependence of all parties to co-construct a shared endeavour. The benefit from collaboration, as opposed to co-operation, is the power to generate creativity, innovation and transformation.

Myth 5: Expertise and growth is lost through collaboration

As a co-construction across individuals and entities, collaboration means breaking down the boundaries between people and the 'silos of expertise'. The fear in breaking these siloed boundaries is that deep expertise is diluted or even lost, supporting the aphorism 'a camel is a horse designed by a committee'. We have already argued that collaboration is only genuine and productive when there is clarity of purpose for the collaboration. Collaboration is based not on consensus but on the emergence of the best ideas through the process of co-constructing and making new connections. Through the shared endeavour, collaboration can maximize the potential of expertise across 'silos' to achieve more effective and more customized outcomes for wider, more complex issues.

In *Smart Collaboration: How Professionals and their Firms Succeed in Breaking Down Silos* (2016), Heidi K. Gardner argues that the global trend towards specialization of expertise in legal firms for example, does not solve the increasingly complex problems of clients. The difficulties of working across the globe with multiple and diverse customers, regulators, competitors, employees, shareholders and local communities requires a more collaborative approach. This comment from Jennifer Daniel, the chief legal officer of Colgate-Palmolive, in a Harvard Law School interview makes the point:[18]

> I can tell you that almost every significant legal issue I have encountered has been multifaceted in nature. It is rare to have a problem that has only one dimension. Solving these complex issues requires individual lawyers to work together … The reality is that the nature of business has changed sufficiently such that work is more complex, more dispersed, and more global. As a result, we are often not looking for the advice of just one lawyer with one set of expertise. I am looking for the advice of many lawyers across a spectrum of jurisdictions and issues. That puts a real premium on collaboration.

Gardner argues that collaboration solves more complex problems, and gives organizations greater success with strategy, sustainability, innovation and profitability. She shows that law firms for example that use multiple practice areas through cross-practice collaboration generate many times more revenue.[19]

Not having collaboration and maintaining silos of expertise can have negative effects, as Gillian Tett[20] argues in *The Silo Effect: The Peril of Expertise and the Promise of Breaking Down Barriers.* Of the 2008 global financial crisis she noted,

> everywhere I looked in the financial crisis it seemed that tunnel vision and tribalism had contributed to the disaster. People were trapped inside their little specialist departments, social groups, teams, or pockets of knowledge. Or, it might be said, inside their silos.[21]

True collaboration explores a diversity of expertise, disciplines and perspective taking, and from that diversity emerges a different way of looking at things that breaks down silos. The Johns Hopkins Community Partnership, for instance, aimed to foster a collaborative team-based culture across health care settings to see things differently through multiple lenses. A collaborative approach more effectively met the health needs of patients, and as a consequence silos in healthcare were broken down. The powering of new thinking, problem solving and better communicating through collaboration demonstrates again the integral connections between the 4Cs.

Collaboration and the other Cs

Although the 4Cs are integrally bound to each other, their relationships reveal a productive tension. Productive tension is a dynamic that gives both friction and momentum to something at the same time. For example, the friction or obstacles that seem to prevent a story from moving forward, the 'cliffhanger moments', paradoxically are the tensions that propel the story forward. We use the tension of paradoxes to explore the complex but symbiotic interrelationships between the intrinsically interdependent 4Cs. It is through the paradox we better understand the dynamic of the relationships. Collaboration and creativity, for instance, can be explored through a tension between divergence and emergence.

Collaboration and creativity: the paradox of divergence and emergence

Collaboration enriches knowledge and growth through the divergent viewpoints brought by individuals (or entities) to the group (or partnerships). The paradox is that with true collaboration, the diversity of ideas and perspectives, rather than be in conflict with each other, lead to the creative process of emergence. Emergence is the phenomenon of something emerging from the interaction of the divergent components in a complex system. In collaborative emergence, ideas flow and emerge unpredictably from the successive individual contributions of the participants in a group or partnership.

Dissonance (difference) in expressed thinking across a group of people leads to something new. Keith Sawyer, psychologist and innovation expert, explains: 'When we collaborate, creativity unfolds across people; the sparks fly faster, and the whole is greater than the sum of its parts. Collaboration drives creativity because innovation always emerges from a series of sparks – never a single flash of insight.'[22] Collaboration sparks creativity and curiosity through the cross-fertilization of divergence and taking different perspectives.[23] It also increases motivation in the group and the taking of chances by 'spreading the risk' to innovate[24] and why that happens is apparent in the next paradox, strength versus vulnerability.

Collaboration and critical reflection: the paradox of vulnerability and strength

By being vulnerable in collaboration (and arguably in many things as social work researcher Brene Brown[25] argues) is not a weakness. Collaboration only works if there is relational trust to take risks and be open to test your own and other's ideas. Being open like this is a form of vulnerability. Vulnerability means tolerating and embracing uncertainty, risk and emotional exposure. It takes critical reflection and awareness of our own and other's vulnerability to allow us to embrace the uncertainty and risk of working with others.

Without being vulnerable, critically reflecting and contesting our own and other's ideas, we cannot truly collaborate. The vulnerability of the critically reflective self, necessary for collaboration and generating new ideas, is a risk mitigated by the strength of numbers in collaboration. New ideas feel less risky in collaboration when the risk is shared by others. The numbers in a group or partnership elicits empowerment, but at the same time, collaboration requires vulnerability for that empowerment.

Collaboration and communication: the paradox of diversity and a common language

All participants or partners in collaboration have to voice or communicate their ideas and perspectives. The diversity of different perspectives is what gives the coming together of individual entities the 'genius' of collaboration. The paradox is that the difference between individual voices has to be unified through a common language, for without a common language we cannot communicate with each other. By common language we mean a language of collaboration that supports the action and agency generated by true communication (see Chapter 7 for the Communication Crystal coherence maker). The common language for collaboration is the process we present in the Collaboration Circles coherence maker. It unifies and demonstrates a common language of communication in collaboration but at the same time promotes communication in diverse and divergent thinking.

A process for collaboration: Collaboration Circles

We have constructed a coherence maker (Figure 8.2) that synthesises what we know about successful collaborations, and helps to guide team members and partnerships through a process of communication and co-constructing the best ideas. We have used the metaphor of circles to describe collaboration.

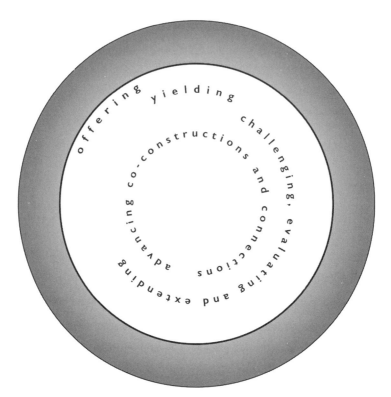

FIGURE 8.2 *Collaboration Circles.*

'Circles' are groups of people with a shared interest. These groups have a strong sense of connectedness and, although they can be viewed as closed cliques, we see circles as having the capacity to intersect and connect with new circles. This is evoked by the epigram:

> He drew a circle that shut me out -
> Heretic, rebel, a thing to flout.
> But love and I had the wit to win:
> We drew a circle and took him In![26]

'Collaboration Circles' is a metaphor for connectedness and inclusion. The word 'Circles' also suggests sitting in the shape of a circle. In a circle there is no need for a hierarchy, all faces can be recognized and all voices can be heard.

The symbol of circles is significant in supporting a conceptual understanding of collaboration. Our coherence maker for Collaboration Circles is:

○ Offering.

○ Yielding.

○ Challenging, evaluating and extending.

○ Advancing co-construction and connections.

Collaboration must have structure and order so multiple voices and ideas in a group or partnership are heard but it must also have flexibility and spontaneity to allow voices and ideas to emerge at any time. This is like improvising with others in music or theatre. Improvisers know that to create 'spontaneously' is to follow the shared rules and conventions or 'language' of a collaborative process. A theatre improviser, explains group improvisation in this way:

Like children, we use the imagination to spontaneously play, making everything up as we go. We find ways of listening to each other, sharing ideas and solving problems; when we don't the playing stops. To improvise productively with each other people need to agree on a set of principles which encourage play. The concept of offer and yield is integral to this process.[27]

Like improvisation and play, collaboration has to allow for the spontaneous collective emergence of perceptions and propositions from the group or partnership. It also has to have a culture of trust and a structure of rules that support the building of jointly constructed ideas. Our coherence maker helps facilitate collaboration by giving order and intention to the listening, sharing, playing, problem-solving and co-ownership of collaborative ideas.

Collaborative Circles is a coherence maker that offers structure and an awareness of the processes of how to collaborate. Once understood and practised, group members and partnerships can mindfully move back and forth through the coherence maker's steps in a recursive and iterative way to deepen the goals of the collaboration. We examine in detail each step of the Collaboration Circles process and discuss how the complexities and advantages of collaborative practice support organizational learning, growth and the generation of new ideas. The coherence maker begins with offering.

Offering

To offer is to be an active participant who initiates an idea or action in a group or partnership. This may be the offer of how the group will organize itself, how it will start, or the first suggestion in solving a problem to develop a new idea. Offers are the foundation of communication and provide a focus and direction for the evolving ideas and actions of the collaboration. Offers require commitment, inclusivity and clarity of purpose, and like 'yields' are made continually throughout the collaborative process. Offering and yielding is a dialogic process where ideas (or actions) are continually interpreted by engaging and being interactive. You have to be able to communicate to offer, but without confidence and influence, the communication of the offer has no effect. Offering is a sophisticated process that necessitates communication, risk and trust.

Collaboration only succeeds with successful communication and each step of the coherence maker develops communication skills, beginning with activating dialogue in an offer. A communicator gives structure to, clarifies and extends their thinking by presenting their ideas to others in a relevant, coherent and engaging way. The communicator has to take into account the group or partnership as an 'audience' and this requires further explanations and justifications, further deepening the communicator's thinking. To make an offer open to the whole group, and relevant to the group's endeavour, is the first step in a sophisticated 'dance' in communicating and developing ideas in collaboration.

An offer is an attempt to be inclusive, clear and generous in launching an idea to be extended and challenged by the rest of the group. To feel open to make an offer is also dependent on relational trust in the group. The notion of everyone sharing the goals, benefits, challenges and risks in a collaborative venture is contingent on trust. Moran and John-Steiner argue:

> Trust consists of respect for another person's different perspective, an expectation of good will, and confidence in the other's ability to contribute to the common purpose ... Trust is the foundation for collaboration that makes possible the development of true sharing, openly negotiated conflict, and a long-term relationship despite the uncertainties and risks.[28]

The 'risk' in making an offer is in trusting the goodwill of the group to consider the offer. Trust and goodwill is engendered in the equality of relational status in the group and equal participation. For organizations, the freedom to explore and challenge as equals is instrumental to collaborative learning and working. Social hierarchies are not conducive to collaboration.[29] Jacob Morgan, head of the Future Organization, argues corporate leaders must work openly to create a culture for collaboration. He says, 'If you don't have an organization where people feel the ability to be vulnerable, to be empathic, to be themselves, then you are not going to have collaboration.'[30] An inclusive and confident offer cannot be made when there are issues of high and low status, dominance and submission in a group. This levelling out of status has enormous ramifications for how organizations approach collaboration. As an individual it requires navigating the tightrope walk of vulnerability and empowerment towards trust and equality with other educators, Helen Storey and Mathilda Marie Joubert describe the process of creative collaboration through an interdisciplinary project involving science, fashion and technology:

> ... collaboration is the necessity to be mutually vulnerable ... Whether you are the instigator of the project of not, there has to be a levelling of personality that goes on. There has to be an authentic acceptance of this

fact, because you both decide to be equal in it. Then you have to take each other to the edge of what you individually thought you were capable of.[31]

Individuals and organizations have to develop skills and understandings in how to contribute, and how to allow others to contribute in the collaborative endeavour. This begins with being cognizant of the generosity, commitment and trust involved in making an offer, and then 'yielding' to the offer. In the J-CHiP healthcare model, the initial patient contact included a 'barriers to care' assessment administered by both the patient and a community health worker. It was an 'offer' to involve the patient in recognizing the obstacles to their healthcare. Holding the assessment in the patient's home gave the patient a greater sense of trust and empowerment to 'yield' and engage with the barriers to care assessment.

Yielding

A yield is the acceptance and development of an offer. Yielding produces or provides something (like a crop produces a yield) in response to an offer. It is not 'submitting' or 'conceding' to an offer, it is to connect, proceed and profit from the offer. Rather than giving way, yielding is being receptive to generate something further. It is not simply saying yes to another offer, it is taking an equal share of responsibility in supporting or shaping the focus of the offer. A yield is 'yes and . . .' or 'yes but . . .' but it is not blocking, shutting down or ignoring someone else's offer. Yielding links or builds your own thinking to someone else's previous offer, even if it means going in a new direction (yes but . . .). Group brainstorming as a process is a multitude of offers and yields. The yield as a response to an offer requires engagement, commitment and elaboration.

Active listening or engaging is critical for communication and collaboration. The nature of attentive listening is that it should lead to hearing your own words echoed through others.[32] Active engagement is developed and realized by repeating others' ideas, asking questions about them, and elaborating on what has been said or done. To yield is to use these components of active engagement. An offer cannot be ignored or rejected so attentive engagement means being able to elaborate and reason with what someone has already said. The communication mechanisms of presenting, explaining, elaborating and reasoning in the offering and yielding of collaboration is when collaborators begin to 'apply' their ideas. Learning in 'how' and 'why' to explain and ask questions encourages collaborators to engage in the higher order collaborative discourse of deeper reasoning.[33]

Offering and yielding is the basis of developing both cognitive (thinking and reasoning) and interpersonal (social) communication skills. Yielding is respecting, engaging and empathising with others by acknowledging their contributions. The socially accommodating behaviours of offering and yielding must not lead, however, to the consensus and conformity of 'group think' (otherwise known as the 'group bubble'). Group think occurs when external feedback is not sought or considered, and the group continually feeds on its own 'rightness' rather than exposing the group to the discipline of external critique and different perspectives. Overcoming 'group think' depends upon the third stage of the Collaboration Circles coherence maker: challenging, evaluating and extending.

Challenging, evaluating and extending

'Group think' describes a 'mode of thinking that people engage in when they are deeply involved in a cohesive in-group'.[34] Group outcomes become constrained when group members strive for unanimity and conformity. The 'strain for consensus' in groups can lead to members fearing or second-guessing reactions from the group. Reluctance to voice dissent leads to conformity in thinking, which inhibits the group's potential for growth.[35] Through fear of difference, adverse reactions and conflict, the 'strain for consensus' can be manifest as a silent or closed reaction of, 'we will have to agree to disagree'. Agreeing to disagree is not collaboration. Indifference is also not a feature of collaboration. 'Challenging and evaluating' is a feature of collaboration as it probes and extends ideas by supporting and encouraging divergent and diverse thinking. It is thinking developed by reflection, debate and understanding using skills in constructive questioning, alternatives, perspective taking, counter-argument, reasoning, persuasion and summarizing.

Collaborators must be aware of a behavioural climate that inculcates group social cohesion as well as individual differences in thinking and working. Free flowing ideas and information, and fluid divisions of labour, are dependent on the fostering of this climate. It is a climate described by leadership and organizational behaviour experts, Isaksen and colleagues' Situational Outlook Questionnaire[36] for creativity and change. The Situational Outlook Questionnaire has been used for many years as a tool to assess the organizational climate that supports change, innovation and creativity. It identifies an atmosphere that engenders challenge/involvement; freedom; trust/openness; idea-time; playfulness and humour; idea-support; debate; and risk-taking. In collaborations there has to be an emotional 'safety zone' within which both support and constructive criticism are effectively practiced.[37] As with the offer, the trust in a group or partnership is paramount for people to take the risk of honest dialogue in challenging, evaluating and extending.

Support and constructive criticism can be practised if people understand that diversity in knowledge, different temperaments and ways of working, all complement and strengthen the capacity of a group's or a partnership's joint purpose. Individual differences or differences between partners have to be recognized as complementary to making up the group's 'whole'. Productive collaborations are made up of individual parts with different perspectives, expertise, resources, needs and talents. This is apparent in the 'barriers to care' assessment example in the Johns Hopkins Community Health Partnership. The personal assessment by the patient and community health worker (an offer and yield) was further evaluated and challenged by a care management assessment system at a clinic where demographic, clinical and health histories were combined with the patient's priorities. This combined health plan was reviewed during team-based visits and extended into a care plan that developed protocols to barriers to care, specific disease issues, behavioural health needs and connected patients and families to community resources. It is a process of offering, yielding, challenging, evaluating and extending through collaboration to meet the best outcomes for the patient.

Challenging, evaluating and extending in the Collaboration Circles coherence maker recognizes and employs different perspectives as strengths to overcome biases and assumptions in default thinking. For some organizations, challenging, evaluating and extending are intuitive, for others these practices require explicit scaffolding[38] into group discussions and idea generation. Naming, exploring and practising these concepts for collaboration creates a culture that values the potential that diverse individuals and entities provide. We have worked with organizations and partnerships that gradually transform and learn to trust the collaborative process and each other, through the openness and integrity of challenging, evaluating and extending.

Commonalities and dissimilarities in groups or partnerships are vital to the enhancement of learning and working. They allow for a 'representational' space for new understandings and possibilities. Research psychologist Vlad Petre Glaveanu[39] argues that collaboration is a fusion of an individual's *personal representational space* and a group's *common representational space*. It is a fusion that gives rise to enrichment and creativity.

It is this common representational space where the group's creative dynamics take place and it is here where different thinking styles collide and by this spark the creative process. All is achieved of course if members communicate with one another, don't withhold information and allow the free flow of ideas, and therefore both intend to share and participate in the construction of a common space.[40]

Moran and John-Steiner claim the foundation and benefits of collaborative practice is in the interaction of different individuals as they challenge, evaluate and extend each other's thinking. The divergence and diversity of thinking produces a creative tension that drives the productivity of collaboration.

> Collaboration's goal is not to reach consensus, as such agreement does not lead to learning or challenge. Not only are tensions between vulnerability and security, doing and getting done, jumping in and stepping back, and collaborators' personal differences not eliminated, but preferably they are taken advantage of as a mechanism for bringing out latent opportunities of the domain.[41]

Through diversity, multiple perspectives and the 'fruitful cultivation of tension', individual assumptions and unexamined beliefs are examined and challenged in collaboration. Challenging creates the spark for latent ideas and opportunities to emerge. Evaluating as a reflective and analytical practice holds up 'mirrors' as feedback of what has been achieved by the group. Through challenge and evaluation in the collaborative process, ideas and actions are constructed and extended to their full potential. It is then there is progress to the final but on-going step in the Collaboration Circles scaffold: advancing co-construction and connections.

Advancing co-construction and connections

Collaboration is more than being co-operative, it is a process to co-construct and connect knowledge that furthers what we already know or do. The act of co-construction is to give shape to the emergent ideas of a group, organization or partnership. A co-construction is to take joint ownership of the process and what has been achieved. Advancing co-construction promotes action that connects the collaboration to future learning and possibilities. Joint ownership or shared meaning-making of the co-construction is critical to collaboration.

Everyone involved in collaboration must identify as being a part of the outcome or end product, or on-going outcome. To identify with the work through ownership is a powerful motivator. The mutual sense of purpose and social cohesion of collaboration encourages the intrinsic motivation and sense of agency to achieve.[42]

In Google's research of essential dynamics for team effectiveness they describe ownership as 'meaning' and team members 'finding a sense of purpose in either the work itself or the output'.[43]

Identity and individual agency is bound up in collaboration but there is a balance between the individual (or entity) losing a sense of self in the group, and the individual (or entity) taking over the identity of the group. The processes of offering and yielding, challenging and evaluating attempt to scaffold a balance between the autonomy and the flexibility of the individual in a group or the entity in a partnership. That is not to say collaboration is without tension and struggle. If the collaborative process is clearly delineated to generate a climate of trust and confidence, the tensions, challenges and struggles, rather than being debilitating, stimulate growth and ways forward.

Collaboration can be a 'dissembling of identity' as you bravely risk your ideas with others.[44] This co-mingling requires opening up to others and working towards solutions rather than seeing the development of ideas with others as a compromise or reductionism. Co-construction should be considered as an opening up to the possibility of something unique between individuals or between larger entities. Storey and Joubert explain that in collaboration:

> you have to be prepared to open up and to truly take that other person into account, and not become prescriptive to them. And that is where the risk is, because they can come up with something that you don't like. The ideal scenario is that you come up with the third idea that neither of you have thought of on your own. There is something about the coming together of

the two of you that produces something that is unique and when it appears it is unquestionably there.[45]

Advancing co-construction and connections clarifies collaboration as not just an agreed goal and product, but a shared experience focusing on the connections between people and partnerships. These collaborations are the stimulation and pleasure of collaboration as an 'affair of the mind' and 'thought community'.[46] For the Johns Hopkins Community Health partnership their collaborations are an on-going thought community. Their aim for patient care is to promote caregiver support with a longitudinal focus on health and positive health habits with the East Baltimore community. Advancing co-constructions and connections for Johns Hopkins Medicine is in continuing to evolve and transform the health and educational practices of their health system. They argue:

> For JHM and its partners, the J-CHiP program is functioning as a potent catalyst for changes needed to promote improved care coordination and has resulted in a very meaningful cultural transformation … Ultimately, true patient, provider and care team engagement will be necessary for sustainable success. As a learning health care system, JHM believes that J-CHiP has advanced its academic mission, stimulated genuine collaboration with the community, and catalyzed true delivery transformation.[47]

Even with technology contracting time and space, collaboration does take time. As an addition to the work itself, time and effort must be provided to facilitate the dynamics and climate of positive relationships and equal participation. The time and energy in collaboration is an investment in enriching and sustaining growth. Through collaboration, organizations have an enormous capacity to ignite and generate ideas across the silos of knowledge, issues and problems to meet the challenges of the future. Or quite simply, in the words of Vera John-Steiner, 'By joining with others we accept their gift of confidence, and through interdependence, we achieve competence and connection. *Together we create our futures.*'[48]

Collaboration starts with:

- *Offering* – initiating and communicating an idea or action for a group's collective endeavour.

- *Yielding* – accepting and developing the offer to generate further ideas and actions.

- *Challenging, evaluating and extending* – probing, analysing and promoting new perspectives to generate and deepen ideas.

- *Advancing co-constructions and connections* – taking joint ownership of the shared endeavour process and continuing to harness the collective genius of a group.

Getting started: building collaboration in organizations

Building genuine collaboration requires an organization to ask the following big questions.

How is 4C collaboration in your organization:

1 Co-constructive

   How are the collaborations a shared endeavour of goals, risk, ideas, relationships and trust?

2 Productive

   How are the organization's collaborations clear and fit for purpose?

3 Taking different perspectives

Where are complex ideas being solved and new ideas generated through perspective-taking in collaborations?

4 Connected

How is collaboration linked to creativity, critical reflection and communication in the organization?

5 Applied

Where and when can the Collaboration Circles coherence maker be implemented and sustained to advance co-constructions and connections?

The next chapter concludes the book by discussing the realities of transformation, offering some strategies to understand and enact real and beneficial change.

9

How 4Cs can close the rhetoric reality gap: some implications

FIGURE 9.1 *The road to transformation.*

We are unapologetically aspirational about the future of organizations. Aspirations are critical for our organizations and our society generally so that we can imagine a future that moves us beyond 'business as usual' models and prepares us for uncertain times. We claim the 4Cs are powerful because they bridge the divide between rhetoric and reality. They enable transformation in tangible ways and if understood deeply within an organization they can lead to dynamic thriving working environments where the 4Cs lead to human flourishing rather than the creeping irrelevance and decline that we have seen in the case studies of Nokia and other organizations. In some cases, we have seen the possibilities when the 4Cs are deeply embedded in an organization's practice (the Glasgow Effect, Lego, IDEO and Dresden Optics).

Transformation, however, is a difficult process that requires a deep understanding of practice and the possibilities of re-imagining that practice. As we have been writing this book we have paid attention to our internal 'critical voices' provoking us; asking us questions, and reminding us of our work in the 'real world'. In this final chapter, we are going to examine the impacts and implications of the transformation on organizations. We also recognize that transformation is a relational human process that happens with real people in real organizations creating complex and difficult problems. Authentic transformation is a collaborative process that only works when teams comprising leaders, employees, owners, shareholders, governors and the community recognize the potential that the 4Cs has for making our organizations better for all. In short, we recognize that transformation has to be realistic as well as hopeful. In the next few pages we want to briefly address some of the issues that have arisen as we have worked with organizations striving for transformation through the 4Cs.

Leading transformation

Transformative leadership is an ongoing process not a one-off or a project focused exercise. As we discussed in Chapter 4, 4C leadership is about embedding the features of the Organizational Effectiveness Wheel in the organization by developing those capacities in individuals and teams.

In this final chapter, we want to revisit the Leading Organizations Framework (LOF) that we introduced in Chapter 3 (Figure 3.4) to emphasize the distributed and iterative qualities of leadership and transformation. We have italicized the features of the OEW in Table 9.1 to demonstrate how the qualities of the OEW contribute directly to leadership throughout an organization. Table 9.1 poses critical questions for organizations to develop distributed leadership that embeds the features of the Leading Organizations Framework (LOF) throughout a transforming organization.

If organizations can embed leadership through their organization by asking these sometimes difficult questions the enablers of transformation will be more useful and well-integrated throughout the organization.

Enabling organizational transformation

Our motivation for writing this book was the need to reconcile the realities of organizations with the urgent need for transformation. As organizations face the shifting present and future, they will need to transform structures, processes and approaches to suit the prevailing conditions. While we do not have a crystal ball we do have the benefit of observation and analysis from organizations who deal with transformation in diverse settings. Deloitte, which has longstanding experience with change management, claim:

> working in teams will likely become the norm in business, and dynamism will become an organizational hallmark. Building and supporting teams

TABLE 9.1 *Embedding the LOF across organizations*

4C Leadership feature	Critical questions for embedding LOF
Vision	• Beyond sharing the vision do individuals and teams have the agency to *influence* implementation of the vision and effectively *communicate* it? • Is there space for *critical reflection* that leads to action from all within the organization?
Structure	• Is there *adaptability* built into the plans and implementation of the structures? Are they inherently flexible and agile while remaining clear? • Do the structures allow for individual and team *creativity* or are they too rigid to allow for creative emergence?
Collaborative partnerships	• Are partnerships based on authentic *collaboration* (not hierarchical)? • Are the partnerships coherent and characterized by clear *communication* and true *collaboration*?
Culture	• Is the leadership based on developing human thriving in the organization and the community through *altruism*? • Does *engagement* and *perseverance* feature throughout the organization as individuals and teams focus on transformation processes?
Strategy and integration	• Are the strategies being designed for transformation *collaborative* to ensure buy in and integration to all ideas and projects throughout the organization? • Do individuals and teams within the organization have the agency to influence the strategies and their integration into the life of the organization?
Learning and evaluation	• Are the learning and evaluation strategies promoting *critical reflection* on the processes and possibilities of transformation? • Do the learning and evaluation strategies develop *creative* responses for the challenges and opportunities that arise from the transformation process?

will be leaders' principal tasks . . . Leading organizations will offer dynamic developmental opportunities for employees to build their careers, while companies that continue to operate in the old manner will likely struggle to keep up. In this new world, more nimble organizations will have certain advantages, but successful large organizations will keep pace by building stronger ecosystems and partnerships that broaden their workforces and capabilities.[1]

Future organizations, according to Deloitte (who of course make their money by implementing change management strategies), are flexible, agile and in many ways totally different from the accepted norms of some of the organizations we have featured (Nokia, VW etc.). In Table 9.2 we have adapted Deloitte's 'old rules' versus 'new rules' and added some transformative enablers that we have discussed here. Table 9.2 details the transformation process enablers that apply to Deloitte's new rules for organizations. These process enablers bring coherence (that is why we call them coherence makers) to the kinds of strategies outlined by Deloitte and go some way to help organizations bridge the gap between rhetoric and reality.

The new rules outlined here are consistent with our experience. Table 9.2 demonstrates these changes require deep transformation in the capacities within organizations. The coherence makers simplify and cohere intangible concepts such as creativity, transformation and leadership. This opens the door to understanding and engaging with the complexity these processes present, but in a framework that all can understand. In reality, these changes depend on the organization's ability to shift focus from hierarchies and 'business as usual' to developing 4C capacities and applying them to the new organizational expectations and structures.

Our main motivation for writing this book was to close the gap between aspiration to transformation in organizations (the rhetoric/reality gap) to demonstrate how authentic and beneficial transformation might be achieved.

TABLE 9.2 *Enablers of transformation*

Old rules	New rules	4C Transformation process enablers
Organized for efficiency and effectiveness	Organized for learning, innovation and customer impact	– Organizational Effectiveness Wheel (OEW) – Deep Learning Diamond – Creativity Cascade – Transformation Tangle coherence maker (introduced in this chapter)
Company viewed as a hierarchy, with hierarchical decision rights, structure and leadership progression	Company viewed as an agile network, empowered by team leaders and fuelled by collaboration and knowledge-sharing	– Collaboration Circles – Critical Reflection Crucible – Communication Crystal
Structure based on business function with functional leaders and global functional groups	Structure based on work and projects, with teams focused on products, customers and services	– Collaboration Circles – Transformation Tangle – 4C Leadership Framework – Deep Learning Diamond
Advancement through promotion upward with many levels to progress through	Advancement through many assignments, diverse experiences, and multifunctional leadership assignments	– 4C Leadership Framework – Critical Reflection Crucible
People 'become leaders' through promotion	People 'create followers' to grow influence and authority	– Collaboration Circles – Organizational Effectiveness Wheel
Culture ruled by fear of failure and perceptions of others	Culture of safety, abundance, and importance of risk-taking and innovation	– Creativity Cascade – Critical Reflection Crucible – Organizational Effectiveness Wheel
Roles and titles clearly defined	Teams and responsibilities clearly defined, but roles and jobs change regularly	– Collaboration Circles – 4C Leading Organization Framework – Deep Learning Diamond – Communication Crystal
Process based	Project-based	– Organizational Effectiveness Wheel – Deep Learning Diamond

Adapted from Deloitte's 'The Organization of the Future: Old rules v's New rules'[2]

While most organizations know what Deloitte have termed the 'new rules' are at least worth considering, implementing them is no easy matter. The coherence makers we present throughout the book, but particularly in Chapters 4–8, are our contribution to closing the gap between aspiration and action for integrating these essential twenty-first century capabilities into the very DNA and culture of organizations. Part of understanding the context for transformation is an understanding of the forces that externally influence organizations, particularly in times of change.

External factors

These external changes are often forced on organizations by the prevailing conditions of postnormality that we referred to in Chapter 2. Chaos, complexity and contradiction[3] have created pressure for change in our society. Our organizations are shaped by these pressures. In the face of this rapid change, one thing is clear to us. We need to articulate a way of transforming, developed through the substantial resources that already exist in organizations, that responds effectively to the needs of the twenty-first century.

We also realize that we need to propose approaches to organizations and individuals (including leaders) that are realistic and possible in diverse industries, sectors and contexts. We are aware that some of the ideas we have here may appear utopian. We do not imagine a perfect future but one of the attractions of utopias are that they are implicitly hopeful as they give us a possible future to 'sail towards'. As Oscar Wilde said:

> A map of the world that does not include Utopia is not worth even glancing at, for it leaves out the one country at which Humanity is always landing. And when Humanity lands there, it looks out, and, seeing a better country, sets sail. Progress is the realisation of Utopias.[4]

In response to overwhelming change, all organizations must navigate towards a better metaphorical 'country'. That is not to say that the 'country' that exists currently is not worthwhile. We think our institutions and organizations (like welfare agencies, hospitals, government organizations and businesses) are often the glue that creates a civilized and democratic society that seeks human flourishing. Nonetheless, and no matter how noble our organizations are, none of them are excluded from the external pressures that are forcing change across our communities. In short, we need a realistic vision of what transformation looks and feels like.

Realistic organization transformation

Transformation is a long and painstaking process that requires patience. Often organizations imagine that what they need is a hero leader to sweep in and change things overnight. While this is a seductive myth, it is rarely the case that change is effective when undertaken with great haste. In the Save the Children Fund International case study (Chapter 4), balance was struck between change that took too long and change that was abrupt. In this case study transformation was expedited as the momentum for change accelerated. This did not happen by accident. The organization collaborated, consulted and patiently pursued transformation by building a shared vision for change at all levels.

Organizations who wish to transform often face issues of intransigence from staff, management, clients/customers, suppliers and sometimes the community. Transformation is perceived as risky. Ironically, as we have discussed, the risk lies in not transforming. Change, or at least sustainable change, takes time, energy and patience, and as such expectations need to be managed. While transformation is different for each organization there are a few patterns that we notice in most cases. The slow pace of organizational change is difficult to accept in some ways. This approach does not offer the 'easy fixes' that some may demand internally and externally. It does, however, recognize that organizations are complex, and that transforming organizations exacerbates that complexity. Our hope is that the model of transformation that we outline here will accomplish two things. Firstly, we hope it gives some sense of the process of transformation required to engage whole organization change with the 4Cs approach. Secondly, and perhaps more critically, we hope that this structure persuades organization leadership teams that change, while difficult and complex, is achievable if that change process is led in a creative, critically reflective, collaborative and openly communicative manner.

What does a transforming 4Cs organization look like?

We think it is worth describing how an organization transformed through the 4Cs approach might look like. The organizations that we have observed transforming effectively have reformed their structures and strategies to make creativity, critical reflection, communication and collaboration the drivers for all of their practices and processes. The organizations have not implemented fringe and irrelevant change; they have fundamentally changed how they work with each other and deliver for their clients, customers etc. The culture in the organizations reflects a qualitative change in relationships that are less hierarchical and more open. These organizations encourage questions to be asked and problems to be posed and responded to.

Problems do not magically disappear in these organizations but the way these problems are managed reflects the 4Cs approach. Instead of fear, people work collaboratively and creatively to manage super complex problems. In short, our argument (in this chapter and throughout this book) is that as individuals transform through the 4Cs, organizations transform to become the 4Cs creative, critically reflective, communicative and collaborative. In other words, as individual capacities (and not just in leadership) begin to develop (often slowly and imperceptibly) the whole culture of an organization will begin to transform in its culture, practice and approach.

TABLE 9.3 *The problem-solving continuum*

CREATIVITY continuum

Awakening	Applying	Accelerating	Advanced	Adept
Attempts to engage with familiar ideas but has difficulties perceiving, reflecting and imagining the possibility of new ideas. Is unsure of the capacity and challenges of creative practice.	Attempts to reflect on and imagine possibilities, but has difficulty exploring iteratively and laterally a number of ideas, and then selecting and refining the best new idea. Shows an awareness of the capacity and challenges of creative practice.	Shows discipline and flexibility in iteratively and laterally reflecting on, playing with and developing new ideas, and attempts to select and refine the best idea for a particular purpose. Is developing reflective and active processes in creative practice.	Is playful, resilient and persistent when exploring, developing and refining possibilities, and uses critically reflective, collaborative and communication processes to discern and evaluate the best ideas and their purpose. Is critically reflective and active in realizing the capacity, challenges and ethical understandings of creative practice.	Tolerates ambiguity and uncertainty to explore the unexpected and unknown, and generates interest and excitement by making new connections and challenging ideas using critically reflective, collaborative and communication processes. Is insightful using critical reflection, ethical reasoning and action to realize the capacity and challenges of creative practice.

CRITICAL REFLECTION continuum

Awakening	Applying	Accelerating	Advanced	Adept
Attempts to identify problems but has difficulty framing and responding to questions that develop thinking processes to find solutions and take action.	Attempts to frame and respond to questions that address identified problems, but has difficulty recognizing assumptions or acting to manage and re-solve problems.	Recognizes assumptions to frame questions and attempts to manage and re-solve problems by contesting and elaborating ideas to make reasoned judgements and decisions to take action.	Reassesses judgements, decisions and actions by contesting and adapting ideas to manage and re-solve problems, and attempts to interrogate the influence of assumptions and power in thinking and acting.	Frames critical questions to explore own and others' judgements, decisions and actions and continues to manage and re-solve problems through reasoning, re-assessment and imagining how assumptions and power can be transformed.

COMMUNICATION continuum

Awakening	Applying	Accelerating	Advanced	Adept
Is unsure of the capacity and challenges of critical reflective practice.	Shows an awareness of the capacity and challenges of critical reflective practice.	Is developing reflective and active processes in critical reflective practice.	Is critically reflective and active in realizing the capacity, challenges and ethical understandings of critical reflective practice.	Is insightful using critical reflection, ethical reasoning and action to realize the capacity and challenges of critical reflective practice.
Attempts to engage with or craft a message but has difficulty being aware of controlling mediums used for making and expressing meaning. Is unsure of the capacity and challenges of communication practice.	Engages with or crafts messages with intent of purpose for an audience but has difficulties making and conveying precise meaning through the control of mediums. Shows an awareness of the capacity and challenges of communication practice.	Enables and crafts messages to convey purpose and attempts to choose and control mediums that engage and connect with an audience with greater precision of meaning. Is developing reflective and active processes in collaborative practice.	Interacts with and enables more sophisticated crafting of messages by choosing and manipulating mediums to create active and connected meaning for an audience. Is critically reflective and active in realizing the capacity, challenges and ethical understandings of communication practice.	Interacts with and generates crafted and complex messages through the manipulation of mediums to create dynamic meaning, action and agency for participants. Is insightful using critical reflection, ethical reasoning and action to realize the capacity and challenges of communication practice.

Messages can be communicated through mediums that are oral, aural, written, read, visual, verbal, non-verbal, spatial, sensory, affective, symbolic, multi-modal, technology.

TABLE 9.3 *Continued*

COLLABORATION continuum

Awakening	Applying	Accelerating	Advanced	Adept
Attempts to communicate with others, but has difficulty negotiating and taking responsibility for a shared understanding of a group's joint purpose.	Engages with others and attempts to negotiate a shared understanding of the group's goals, but has difficulties taking responsibility and influencing the outcome of the joint venture.	Is committed to reflecting on and influencing the outcome of the group's joint purpose, but needs to support the group's direction by challenging and evaluating to deepen the outcomes.	Contributes to challenging and evaluating the group's free-flowing ideas leading to productive outcomes, but possibilities could be explored further by extending ideas and connections in the group's shared endeavour.	Is highly motivated in fostering and opening up possibilities, and allows ideas to emerge and take form into action that is co-constructed and leads to further connections and agency through the group's shared endeavour.
Is unsure of the capacity and challenges of collaborative practice.	Shows an awareness of the capacity and challenges of collaborative practice.	Is developing reflective and active processes in collaborative practice.	Is critically reflective and active in realizing the capacity, challenges and ethical understandings of collaborative practice.	Is insightful using critical reflection, ethical reasoning and action to realize the capacity and challenges of collaborative practice.

What does 4C transformation feel like?

As we have discussed, a large part of organizational transformation is relational. Strategies and approaches are necessary but there are human and emotional dimensions to this change. We have constructed a coherence maker we call the Transformation Tangle (see Figure 9.2) to outline the stages of transformation and provide a sense of what people might be feeling and thinking as they undertake transformation. We have used the rather untidy metaphor of the tangle, with its twists, turns, knots and difficulties to acknowledge the untidiness of this process. We have been inside countless transformations as observers, participants and facilitators. These transformations are frequently messy, difficult and painful for those inside them. However, if we understand the processes, it makes it easier for us to chart a course through this rough terrain. The best transformations are not 'done to people', they are done with people. Yet no matter how collaborative the approach, transformation often produces fear, anxiety, confusion and stress. The coherence maker we outline here is not a recipe and even though it has phases, they do not all happen at the same time. In any change process, people will approach the transformation and respond differently at different times. The Transformation Tangle is based on research undertaken by American sociologist Jack Mezirow. In his research, he found ten phases for transformative learning.[5] They are:

1   A disorienting dilemma.

2   Self-examination with feelings of guilt or shame.

3   A critical assessment of assumptions.

4   Recognition that one's discontent and process of transformation are shared and that others have negotiated a similar change.

5   Exploration of options for new roles, relationships and actions.

6 Planning a course of action.

7 Acquisition of knowledge and skills for implementing one's plans.

8 Provisionally trying out new roles.

9 Building of competence and self-confidence in new roles and relationships.

10 A re-integration into one's life on the basis of conditions dictated by one's new perspective.

Transformation, in Mezirow's terms, requires deep and difficult emotional work. This approach also requires the individual to actively reflect, develop new skills and trial new approaches that respond to new internal and external pressures and demands. In our view, transformation requires a deep and active understanding of the 4Cs, but particularly Critical Reflection and Creativity to deal with this long and sometimes difficult process. In many of the organizations we have worked with, these kinds of transformation processes can take up to six years and during that time people within organizations have a range of feelings and attitudes towards the transformation (sometimes simultaneously). The Transformation Tangle is an adaptation of Mezirow's approach, based on our experience of transformation processes. Critically, transformation should not be considered a 'one off experience'. It is rather an ongoing and constant feature of a dynamic organization.

The Transformation Tangle

1. Disorientation

In this phase, nothing seems particularly clear about the transformation process. Leaders can outline a clear vision but in most organizations surprise, speculation and anxiety can overtake any kind of vision statement.

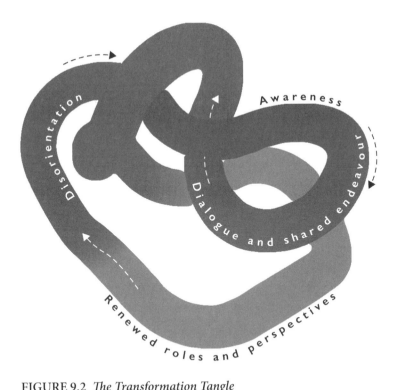

FIGURE 9.2 *The Transformation Tangle*

Disorientation is also present for those thinking about the possibilities of transformation. The process of questioning deeply held assumptions in organizations feels, for many, deeply unsettling. It is, however, critical that everything is 'made strange' so the assumptions which have become 'part of the furniture' can be examined deeply. The ambiguity of disorientation, while unnerving, allows ideas and anxieties to surface which can then facilitate the emergence of more detailed strategies. Wise organizations lessen the effect of disorientation by involving all involved in focused dialogue and a vision that makes the transformation a shared endeavour and not just a management level or top down adventure. In this phase, confusion requires those involved in the transformation to critically reflect in a way that generates opportunities rather than focusing only on the difficulties and obstacles.

2. Awareness

As organizations become aware of the assumptions and then begin the process of re-imagining how activities, approaches and processes might be re-imagined, awareness moves from understanding to opportunity. Awareness begins to emerge as organizations start working out the details of the transformation through the process of re-imagining. In the awareness phase individuals are beginning to understand the need, drivers and the processes for change. Often, they have begun to understand that organizational change necessarily involves personal change. Many individuals are able to begin imagining themselves in new contexts and new roles without understanding all of the details or the implications. In this phase, those leading the transformation must outline clearly the rationale for change. If the rationale is not based on evidence or lacks clarity, anxiety can take hold and dominate discussions. While there will always be a level of anxiety around change, outlining a vison that is inclusive and allows personal agency throughout the organization is likely to facilitate an understanding of each individual's role within the change process. At this point, clear communication that invites questioning and problem and solution discussions can build a shared sense of direction that leads to the next stage in the transformation process.

3. Dialogue and shared endeavour

In this phase of the transformation process, real and authentic consultation occurs. At this phase, all of the 4Cs should be apparent in the discussions and action as transformation moves from discussion to action. We are not referring here to the kind of token consultation which has now become commonplace. This 'consultation for consultation's sake' approach can be damaging for organizations as it builds resentment and cynicism rather than hope and optimism. As organizations talk through the issues and concerns, shared endeavour can be developed to create transformation that is owned by everyone. The Glasgow Effect case study in Chapter 7 is a good example of how a whole community can work across organizational boundaries by using collaborative and non-hierarchical processes to deliver meaning and sustainable benefits for their communities, clients and employees. For this stage to be successful, participants must be taking a part in the action (not just the discussion) of transformation in a way that gives them control (agency). This stage is critical if transformation is to be 'owned' by the whole organization and not just a plaything of management.

4. Renewed roles and perspectives

This means seeing the organization differently – it is a shift in the frame of reference to see the work through the frames of the 4Cs. Once the transformation strategy, approach and understanding is developed, individuals focus on developing capacities in creativity, critical reflection, collaboration and communication. They will continue to develop new perspectives and new ways of working. In a way, this is the 'stuff' of 4C transformation. It is not just a case of changing job titles and where people sit in the office. Authentic transformation is the move from old assumptions, old practices and approaches to transformed 4C capacities.

This will also mean that some within the organization leave. In our experience people who do not wish to engage the transformative practices choose to go elsewhere without too much persuasion. This leaves space for organizations to reconfigure what they do to make their organization more focused on current needs, rather than outmoded practices and processes.

The phases of transformation that we have outlined in the Transformation Tangle do not necessarily happen in a fixed order and like any coherence maker the phases overlap and intersect. We have selected the tangle image to suggest that these phases rarely occur in the uniform manner. At times organizations might get stuck at one of the stages. For example, it is quite common for organizations to pass through the disorientation phase and get stuck in the awareness phase. Often this occurs because the initial emotional energy has dissipated and the momentum for transformation stalls. If this occurs, organizations should critically reflect on whether the dialogue and shared endeavour phase should be revisited. Leaders who are managing these transformations can respond effectively by critically reflecting on the processes, identifying the problems and acting to ensure movement to the next phase. While maintaining momentum is critical there are other realities, or as we have called them here, implications that influence the nature and speed of transformation.

Implications for transformation

The following list of the implications are in no particular order. These implications emerge from our own experience and reflects what we have noticed about transformation and its impacts. This list is not exhaustive but it will provide a 'rough guide' to prepare the traveller for this transformative journey.

Implication 1: Transformed organizations will implement and become the 4Cs

The changes we have discussed in this book are not just about changes to some practices in isolation from the rest of the organization. Organizations that deeply understand the 4Cs will need to change the shape of much of what they do. Capacities such as creativity, critical reflection, communication and collaboration are not only relevant as individual skills for team members and organizational leadership, they need to become part of the culture. For instance, effective organizations that foster creativity will include structures, strategies, policies and leadership that explicitly models creative processes and practices in delivering for its employees, clients, students, shareholders or the public.

Often in our work we hear the claim 'the 4Cs are fine in theory but we don't have the time'. We recognize that organizations are often very busy places and that authentic transformation takes time and energy. It requires organizations to critically reflect upon all the processes, products and approaches and then identify priorities (in the same way Lego did, see Chapter 1). Many of the organizations we have worked with waste time and resources on tasks that do not really contribute to efficiency or productivity or align with their values. The time taken to implement the 4Cs is likely to bring deep benefits for some of the functions organizations see currently as critical. For instance, taking time for critical reflection will assist everyone in organizations (and particularly those with leadership responsibilities) to consider what actually contributes to the quality of the work environment. In short, organizations need to not only develop the 4Cs in their employees they need to *be* the 4Cs. Organizations that transform in this way make the 4Cs a standard expectation for everyone inside and outside the process.

Implication 2: Leadership in organizations will change

In our view leaders do not just have the title leader, manager, CEO or CFO. They are, rather, any member of staff that has the vision, energy and courage to engage with the transformation required in organizations. In most cases this will necessarily involve the head of the organization (with whatever title they take) but will also involve mid-level management and other staff. In essence, a leader is anyone who understands their role as an agent of organizational change. This kind of organizational leadership follows the learning principles we have described: namely transformational leadership is creative, critically reflective, communicative and collaborative. We have deliberately avoided hero narratives here of leaders who come in and turn around failing organizations into 'hero organizations'. As educator Michael Fullan argues:

Charismatic leaders inadvertently often do more harm than good because, at best, they provide episodic improvement followed by frustrated or despondent dependency. Superhuman leaders also do us another disservice: they are role models who can never be emulated by large numbers. Deep and sustained reform depends on many of us, not just on the very few who were destined to be extraordinary.[6]

For the 4Cs to be embedded within organizations, deep cultural change is required. While a talented and capable leader can inspire, initiate, instigate and enable that transformation, it can only be sustained if the culture of the organization collaboratively transforms.

The approach we have described here (the 4Cs) is not a 'fly in fly out', one off, one visit approach. The 4Cs change radically and deeply how organizations work. Fullan argues organizations (he is talking here about education but it applies to many organizations) are beset with 'one off' and frequently contradictory initiatives, policies and approaches that do not create coherent or meaningful transformation: 'the main problem is not the absence of innovation but the presence of too many disconnected, episodic, piecemeal, superficially adorned projects'.[7] Authentic 4C transformation will overarch and underpin and bring all aspects of the organization together to combine aspiration with reality. In other words this is not a project, it is a way of organizational life. We believe (based on our experience of sustainable transformation) that organizations are changed by creative, critically reflective, communicative and collaborative teams rather than charismatic or 'hero' individuals. The individual reformer superheroes may exist, but we are still yet to meet them.

Implication 3: Organizations will focus on 'small data' as well as 'metrics'

The current preference organizations have for metrics has the potential to set distorted priorities. By metrics we mean measures of performance applied to individuals or teams within an organization. As we mentioned the 'small data' (discussed in Chapter 4) such as adaptability, perseverance, influence, collaboration, creativity and communication are resistant to easy measurement. They are de-emphasized when there are easily measurable outcomes such as successful sales, phone calls, key stroke or number of operations undertaken. Recently, historian Jerry Z. Muller argued in *The Tyranny of Metrics*,[8] that our society has become obsessed with valuing metrics to our collective detriment:

> Call it a meme, a discourse, a paradigm, or a fashion. I call it metric fixation. It affects the way people talk about the world, and thus how they think and how they act. The key components of metric fixation are:
>
> - the belief that it is possible and desirable to replace judgement, acquired by experience and talent, with numerical indicators based upon standardized data;
> - the belief that making such metrics public assures that institutions are carrying out their purposes;
> - the belief that the best way to motivate people is by attaching rewards and penalties to their measured performance.
>
> These assumptions have been on the march for several decades, and their assumed truth goes marching on.[9]

We are not arguing for the abolition of metrics but rather a critical reflection on whether all the metrics we create in organizations are meaningful and lead to wisdom and learning or unethical behaviour and poor decision making. There are many recent examples of unethical behaviour emerging when individuals and organizations become motivated by metrics associated with commissions and promotions. Some individuals within financial institutions during the Global Financial Crisis and more recently have made unethical and/or unwise decisions driven by these metrics and have broken or bent the law bringing huge reputational and financial damage to their organizations. Again, there is nothing wrong with rewarding productive work, however, this approach must be balanced against the meaningfulness of the metrics and their contribution to the wellbeing of the organization and the community generally. Muller argues 'The hazard of metrics so purely focused on monetary considerations is that, like so many metrics, they influence behavior.'[10]

Metrics have a part to play in analysing the effectiveness of organizations and to support the development of individuals. An overemphasis can at best distort the vision of an organization and at worst can lead to a culture of unethical behaviour. The problems arise when metrics are considered a panacea for system improvement and without a clear understanding of the organization's context, culture and vision (often by external consultants).

We think that the 4Cs offer abundant possibility to restore the balance for organizations. The coherence makers that we have developed provide a way to refocus organizations on what makes them effective *and* wise. While these features may be more difficult to build metrics around, they are critical for organizations to transform in ways that are not only productive and effective but are also wise.

Changes in the way we evaluate effectiveness will change practice in organizations. You have probably heard the saying 'what matters gets tested'. At the moment in many cases, what gets 'tested' or valued is a very narrow band of understanding, potentially disenfranchising and discouraging valuable team members who have skills that are outside the reach of metrics. Rather, organizations need to develop evaluation practices that integrate this knowledge with the broader skills individuals and organizations require for the challenges they face in the present and into the future.

Implication 4: Organizational practices will be re-imagined

Before organizations embark on 4C transformation they should pause and reflect, as the implications of these changes are not trivial. Our mission in this book has been to demonstrate that, when organizations engage with the 4Cs, everything changes. In the end this means that practices we may feel comfortable and safe with may also have to be re-imagined. In our experience, this can lead to some grieving as people mourn the passing of the ways that we used to do things. On the other hand, what we find in many cases is excitement around the new possibilities that creativity, critical reflection, collaboration and communication make possible. This is apparent in the Glasgow Effect. While some mourned the passing of familiar practices, others saw the opportunity to create authentic and effective transformation by re-imagining how institutions and organizations might work more effectively with the community. The dividend in Glasgow is undeniable. So, while there may be nostalgia for outmoded practices, the re-imagining that transformation brings can deliver strong benefits for our communities, clients and customers.

Making Organizations Relevant through the 4Cs

Relevance for organizations is no longer guaranteed in a world where the old 'normalities' have ebbed away. When we leave behind the sometimes-comfortable traditions that suited another age and reset our organization to meet emerging needs, we might find that they can make a more effective contribution to human flourishing. Our world is made up of many formal and informal organizations, so in our view the extent to which we can transform them to retain their relevance is critical to how we can continue to flourish together.

NOTES

Foreword

1 Lyons, G. (2014) *The Consolations of Economics*, London, Faber & Faber

2 In economics, gross value added (GVA) is the measure of the value of goods and services

3 Hunt, V. Layton, D. Prince, S (2014) *Diversity Matters*, New York, McKinsey and Company

4 Fan, J. (2018) *Delivering Modernity* in: The New Yorker July 23rd 2018

5 Berlin, I. (2014) The Hedgehog and the Fox: An Essay on Tolstoy's View of History, London, W&N

6 Amabile, T. M. (1983). *The social psychology of creativity*, New York, Springer-Verlag.

7 Goleman, D. (2007) *Social Intelligence: The New Science of Human Relationships*, London, Arrow

8 Stiglitz, J. E., & Greenwald, B. C. (2014). *Creating a learning society: A new approach to growth, development, and social progress.* Columbia University Press.

9 Csikszentmihalyi, M. (1996). *Creativity. Flow and the psychology of discovery and invention*, New York: Harper Collins

10 Manville, B. and Ober, J. (2003) *A Company of Citizens*, Boston Mass: Harvard Business School Press.

11 Dweck, C (2012) *Business: Mindset and Leadership*. In: Mindset : How you can fulfil your potential, London, Robinson

12 Axon, L Friedman E, Jordan K (2015) *Learning now: Critical Capabilities for a Complex World*, Cambridge Mass, Harvard Business Publishing http://www.harvardbusiness.org/sites/default/files/19309_CL_LeadershipCap_Paper_July2015_0.pdf

Introduction

1 Sardar, Z. (2010). Welcome to postnormal times. *Futures* 42(5).

Chapter 1

1 'Rocket Car Flies, Then Falls'. *The New York Times*, 6 October, 1979. Retrieved from https://www.nytimes.com/1979/10/06/archives/rocket-car-flies-then-falls.html

2 This is Michael's recollection although Miranda did occasionally play with Lego as well.

3   Cordon, C., Seifert, R. and Wellian, E. (2010). 'The Case Study: Lego'. *Financial Times*, 24 November. Retrieved from https://www.ft.com/content/05806aa4-f819-11df-8875-00144feab49a

4   Lindström, M. (2016). 'Here's How an Old Pair of Sneakers Saved Lego'. *Fortune*, 13 March. Retrieved from http://fortune.com/2016/03/13/heres-how-an-old-pair-of-sneakers-saved-lego/

5   Cordon, C., Seifert, R. and Wellian, E. (2010). 'The Case Study: Lego'.

6   Trangbæk, R. (2017). 'The LEGO Group Reports Record Revenue in 2016'. 9 March. Retrieved from https://www.lego.com/en-us/aboutus/news-room/2017/march/annual-results-2016

7   'Giving Back to Communities'. Retrieved from https://www.lego.com/es-es/aboutus/responsibility/caring-ethical-and-transparent/local-community-engagement, 24 September 2015.

8   Cordon, C., Seifert, R. and Wellian, E. (2010). 'The Case Study: Lego'.

9   Bromley, P. and Meyer, J. W. (2017). 'They are all organizations': The cultural roots of blurring between the nonprofit, business, and government sectors. *Administration & Society* 49(7), 939–66.

10 Senge, P. (1990). *The Fifth Discipline: The Art and Practice of the Learning Organization*. New York: Currency Doubleday.

11 Ibid., p. 9.

12 Ibid., p. 9.

13 Prokesch, S. E. (1997). Unleashing the power of learning: an interview with British Petroleum's John Browne. *Harvard Business Review* 77(5), 148.

14 Newport, C. (2015). *Deep Work: Rules for Focused Success in a Distracted World*. London: Hachette.

15 Ibid., p. 13.

16 Ibid., p. 79.

17 Weaver, G. R. (2006). Virtue in organizations: moral identity as a foundation for moral agency. *Organization Studies* 27(3), 341–68.

18 Alvesson, M. and Spicer, A. (2016). *The Stupidity Paradox: The Power and Pitfalls of Functional Stupidity at Work*. London: Profile Books, p. 4

Chapter 2

1   Martin, R. and Püschel, L. (2015, 2 December). 'Die Another Day: What Leaders Can Do About the Shrinking Life Expectancy of Corporations'. Boston Consulting Group. Retrieved from https://www.bcg.com/publications/2015/strategy-die-another-day-what-leaders-can-do-about-the-shrinking-life-expectancy-of-corporations.aspx

2 Ibid., n.p.

3 Doz, Y. and Wilson, K. (2017). *Ringtone: Exploring the Rise and Fall of Nokia in Mobile Phones*. Oxford: Oxford University Press.

4 Ibid., p. 3.

5 Huy, Q. (2015, 22 September). 'Who Killed Nokia? Nokia Did'. *INSEAD Knowledge*. Retrieved from https://knowledge.insead.edu/strategy/who-killed-nokia-nokia-did-4268#euOlJqAqPWoz0feh.99

6 Ibid., n.p.

7 Ibid., n.p.

8 Bauman, Z. (2005). Education in liquid modernity. *The Review of Education, Pedagogy, and Cultural studies* 27(4), 303–17.

9 Greene, M. (1995). *Releasing the Imagination: Essays on Education, the Arts, and Social Change*. San Francisco: Jossey-Bass.

10 Ibid., p.

11 Komporozos-Athanasiou, A. and Fotaki, M. (2015). A theory of imagination for organization studies using the work of Cornelius Castoriadis. *Organization Studies* 36(3), 321–42.

12 Ibid., p. 322.

13 Marshall, B. K. and Picou, J. S. (2008). Postnormal science, precautionary principle, and worst cases: the challenge of twenty-first century catastrophes. *Sociological Inquiry* 78(2), p. 230.

14 Lim, R. (2012, 23 May). 'Singapore Wants Creativity not Cramming'. *BBC News*, Singapore. Retrieved from http://www.bbc.com/news/business-17891211

15 Sardar, Z. (2010). Welcome to postnormal times. *Futures* 42(5), 435.

16 Ringland, G. (2010). Frameworks for coping with post-normal times: a response to Ziauddin Sardar. *Futures* 42(6), 634.

17 Marshall, B. K. and Picou, J. S. (2008). Postnormal science, p. 243.

18 Eisenhower Study Group (2011). *The Costs of War since 2001: Iraq, Afghanistan, and Pakistan*. Providence: Watson Institute, Brown University.

19 Plumer, B. (2013). 'Nine facts about Terrorism in the United States since 9/11'. *The Washington Post*. Retrieved from https://www.washingtonpost.com/news/wonk/wp/2013/09/11/nine-facts-about-terrorism-in-the-united-states-since-911/

20 Goggin, G. (2006). *Cell Phone Culture: Mobile Technology in Everyday Life*. United Kingdom: Routledge.

21 Baker, S. A. (2012). From the criminal crowd to the 'mediated crowd': the impact of social media on the 2011 English riots. *Safer Communities* 11(1), 40–49.

22 Ibid., p. 45.

23 Sardar, Z. (2010). Welcome to postnormal times, p. 439.

24 Since Osborne and Frey produced their research there have been frequent critiques of their modelling that provide a different view of the future. For instance, Borland, J. and Coelli, M. (2017) Are robots taking our jobs? *Australian Economic Review* 50(4), 377–97. Whatever the case most commentators agree that there are clear and sometimes dramatic changes occurring in the way of working because many industries and professions, such as law, agriculture and business services, have seen the re-shaping of entry level roles. This has made the access to professions and careers somewhat different.

25 Frey, C. B. and Osborne, M. A. (2017). The future of employment: how susceptible are jobs to computerisation? *Technological Forecasting and Social Change* 114, 254–80.

26 Ibid., p. 303.

27 Frey, C. B. and Osborne, M. A. (2017). The future of employment, pp. 254–80.

28 Sardar, Z. (2010). Welcome to postnormal times, p.

29 Frey, C. B. and Osborne, M. A. (2017). The future of employment, pp. 254–80.

Chapter 3

1 Reinhardt, F. L. and Beard, A. (2016). Case study: Dealing with Drought. *Harvard Business Review* 64(11), 105–9.

2 Website for Woolf Farming and Producing. Retrieved from http://www.woolffarming.com

3 Gardner, H. (2007). *Five Minds for the Future*. Boston, MA: Harvard Business Press.

4 Collins, J. and Porras, J. I. (1994). *Built to Last: Successful Habits of Visionary Companies*. New York: HarperBusiness.

5 Ekvall, G. (1991). 'The organizational culture of idea-management: a creative climate for the management of ideas'. In J. Henry and D. Walker (eds), *Managing Innovation* London: Sage pp. 73–9.

6 Schein, E. (2010). *Organizational Culture and Leadership*. San Francisco: Jossey-Bass.

7 Fullan, M. (2014). *Leading in a Culture of Change: Personal Action Guide and Workbook*. San Francisco, CA: Jossey-Bass, p. 53.

8 Alvesson, M. and Spicer, A. (2016). *The Stupidity Paradox: The Power and Pitfalls of Functional Stupidity at work*. London: Profile Books.

9 *Yes, Prime Minister* (1986). BBC (13/2/1986), S1, Ep.6 'A Victory for Democracy'.

10 Alvesson, M. and Spicer, A. (2016). *The Stupidity Paradox*, p. 147.

11 Mintzberg, H. (1994). *The Rise and Fall of Strategic Planning*. New York: The Free Press.

12 Wenger, E. (1998). *Communities of Practice: Learning, Meaning and Identity*. Cambridge: Cambridge University Press.

13 Koongsbakk, N. and Rooney, D. (2017). 'Too busy to learn: Wisdom, mindfulness and grounding learning.' In W. Kupers and O. Gunnlaugson (eds.), *Wisdom Learning: Perspectives on Wising-up Business and Management Education*. London and New York: Routledge, pp. 117–39.

14 Fiorelli, L. and Mayer, R. E. (2015). *Learning as a Generative Activity: Eight Learning Strategies that Promote Understanding*. New York: Cambridge University Press.

15 Costandi, M. (2016). *Neuroplasticity*. The MIT Press Essential Knowledge Series. Cambridge MA: MIT Press, pp. 145–7.

16 Illeris, K. (2009). *Contemporary Learning Theories: Learning theorists . . . in their Own Words*. London: Routledge, p. 14.

17 Turban, S., Freeman, L. and Waber, B. (2017). A study used sensors to show that men and women are treated differently at work. *Harvard Business Review*. Retrieved from https://hbr.ora/2017/10/a-study-used-sensors-to-show-that-men-and-women-are-treated-differently-at-work

18 A sociometric badge or sociometer is a wearable, electronic device used to quantitatively measure social relationships. It can automatically measure face-to-face interaction, conversational time, physical proximity to other people, and physical activity levels using social signals derived from vocal features, body motion and relative location.

19 Mezirow, J. (1997). *Transformative Learning: Theory to Practice*. San Francisco, CA: John Wiley and Sons.

20 Mezirow, J. (2009). *Transformative Learning in Practice: Insights from Community, Workplace and Education*. San Francisco, CA: Jossey-Bass.

21 Rodrigues, F., Pina e Cunha, M., Rego, A. and Clegg, S. (2017). 'The seven pillars of paradoxical organizational wisdom'. In W. Kupers and O. Gunnlaugson (eds), *Wisdom Learning: Perspectives on Wising-up Business and Management Education*. London and New York: Routledge, pp. 98–116.

22 Ibid., p. 109.

23 Sawyer, K. (2015). A call to action: The challenges of creative teaching and learning. *Teachers College Record* 117(10), 1–34.

24 Bilton, C. and Cummins, S. (2014). *Handbook of Management and Creativity*. Cheltenham: Edward Elgar, p. 8.

25 Buell, R. W. and Otazo, A. (2016). 'IDEO: Human-Centred Service Design', case study. Harvard Business School, p. 10. Retrieved from http//hbr.org/product/IDEO-Human-Centered-Serv/an/615022-PDF-ENG

26 Lengnick-Hall, C. A. and Inocencio-Gray, J. L. (2013). Institutionalized organizational learning and strategic renewal: the benefits and liabilities of prevailing wisdom. *SAGE Journal of Leadership and Organizational Studies* 10(4), 420–35.

27 Rodrigues, F., Pina e Cunha, M., Rego, A. and Clegg, S. (2017). The seven pillars of paradoxical organizational wisdom, pp.105–6.

28 House, R. J., Hanges, P. J., Javidan, M., Dorfman, P. W. and Gupta, V. (eds) (2004). *Culture, Leadership, and Organizations: The GLOBE Study of 62 Societies.* Thousand Oaks, CA: Sage.

29 Sawyer, K. (2007). *Group Genius: The Creative Power of Collaboration.* New York: Basic Books.

30 *Milwaukee Business Journal* interview with Steve Wozniak. Retrieved from https://www.theguardian.com/technology/2014/jul/08/steve-wozniakr-steve-jobs-apple

31 *Yes, Prime Minister* (1982). BBC (25/11/1982), S3, Ep.3, 'The Skeleton in The Cupboard'.

32 Orwell, George (1946). 'Politics and the English language'. In P. Davison (ed.), *Orwell and Politics*, London: Penguin Books, p. 407.

33 Sternberg, R. J. (2003). *Wisdom, Intelligence and Creativity Synthesized.* New York: Cambridge University Press, p. 115.

34 Ibid., p. 99.

35 McKenna, B. (2017). 'Embodying a wise graduate disposition in business school education in Wisdom Learning'. In W. Kupers and O. Gunnlaugson (eds), *Wisdom Learning: Perspectives on Wising-up Business and Management Education.* London and New York: Routledge, p.57.

Chapter 4

1 Save the Children International (2016). *Rising to The Challenge.* Save the Children Annual Report, Retrieved from https://www.savethechildren.net/annualreview/ui/docs/Save_the_Children_Annual_Report_2016.pdf, p. 3.

2 Ibid., p. 2.

3 Ibid., p. 7.

4 Baker, C., Chirumberro, F. and Green, L. (2013, 11 July). 'Managing Change at Save the Children'. Boston Consulting Group. Retrieved from https://www.bcg.com/en-au/publications/2013/change-management-organization-design-managing-change-at-save-the-children.aspx

5 Save the Children International (2016). *Rising to the Challenge*, p. 8.

6 Dyer, A., Freeland, G., Gunby, S. and DeTar, T. (2011). 'Leading Transformation Conversations with Leaders on Driving Change'. Boston Consulting Group. Retrieved

from http://image-src.bcg.com/Images/BCG_Leading_Transformation_Oct_2011_
tcm9-110019.pdf, p. 41.

7   Ibid., p. 57.

8   Ibid., p. 42.

9   Ward, J. and Uhl, A. (2012). 'Success and Failure in Transformation: Lessons from 13
    Case Studies'. *360° – The Business Transformation Journal* 3, 30–37.

10 Johnson, E. (2017, 13 June). 'How to Communicate Clearly During Organizational
    Change'. *Harvard Business Review*. Retrieved from https://hbr.org/2017/06/how-to-
    communicate-clearly-during-organizational-change

11 Dyer, A., Freeland, G., Gunby, S. and DeTar, T. (2011). 'Leading Transformation
    Conversations', p. 43.

12 Ibid.

13 Ahlbäck, K., Fahrbach, C., Murarka, M. and Salo, O. (2017, 1 October). 'How to Create
    an Agile Organization'. Survey by McKinsey and Company. Retrieved from https://
    www.mckinsey.com/business-functions/organization/our-insights/how-to-create-an-
    agile-organization

14 Pellegrino, J. and Hilton, M. (2012). *Education for Life and Work: Developing
    Transferable Knowledge and Skills in the 21st Century*. Washington, DC: The National
    Academies Press.

15 Almlund, M., Duckworth, A. L., Heckman, J. J. and Kautz, T. (2011). 'Personality
    Psychology and Economics'. In. E. A. Hanushek, S. Machin and L. Wößmann (eds),
    Handbook of the Economics of Education. Amsterdam: Elsevier, pp. 1–181.

16 Ibid., pp. 6–20.

17 Katz, D. and Kahn, R. L. (1978). *The Social Psychology of Organizations.* New York: Wiley.

18 Roberts, B. W., Walton, K. E. and Viechtbauer, W. (2006). Patterns of mean-level change
    in personality traits across the life course: a meta-analysis of longitudinal studies.
    Psychological Bulletin 132, 3–27.

19 Ibid.

20 Dweck, C. S. (2016). *Mindset: The New Psychology of Success* New York: Ballentine
    Books. p. 7.

21 Ibid.

22 Reid, M. (2011). 'Behind the "Glasgow Effect"'. *WHO* 89(10). Retrieved from http://
    www.who.int/bulletin/volumes/89/10/11-021011/en/

23 Swan, N. (2018). *The Glasgow Effect: Unpacking Why the West of Scotland has Poor
    Health Outcomes.* [Podcast.] Retrieved from http://www.abc.net.au/radionational/
    programs/healthreport/unravelling-the-glasgow-effect/9484600#transcript

24 Ibid.

25 Ibid.

26 Ibid.

27 Ibid.

28 Ibid.

29 Ibid.

30 Ibid.

31 Mezirow, J. (1998). On critical reflection. *Adult Education Quarterly, Sage Journal* 48(3), 185–98.

32 Dewey, J. (1938). *Experience & Education.* New York: Kappa Delta Pi.

33 Mezirow, J., Taylor, E. W. and associates (2009). *Transformative Learning in Practice: Insights from Community, Workplace and Education.* California: Jossey-Bass.

34 Ibid.

35 Lave, J. and Wenger, E. (1991). *Situated Learning: Legitimate Peripheral Participation.* Cambridge: Cambridge University Press.

36 Deep learning is needed to develop individual and organizational capacities in the OEW. At the same time the capacities in the OEW are needed for deep learning. Processes and capacities in the Deep Learning Diamond and the OEW relate to and affect each other in a self-perpetuating feedback loop.

Chapter 5

1   Statistica (1 May, 2017). *How Many People (Aapproximately) Wear Spectacles?* Retrieved from https://www.statista.com/statistics/711514/individuals-who-wear-spectacles-in-selected-european-countries/

2   Dresden (2018). *Our Mission.* Retrieved from https://dresden.com.au/our-story/

3   Grandview Research (2018*). Eyewear Market Size, Share & Trends Analysis Report By Product (Contact Lenses, Spectacles, Plano Sunglasses), By Region (North America, Europe, Asia Pacific, South America, MEA), And Segment Forecasts, 2018–2024.* Retrieved from https://www.grandviewresearch.com/industry-analysis/eyewear-industry

4   Ibid.

5   Asian Development Bank (2014). *Creative Productivity Index: Analysing Creativity and Innovation in Asia.* Retrieved from https://www.adb.org/publications/creative-productivity-index-analysing-creativity-and-innovation-asia

6   IBM (2010, 18 May). *Redefining Competition Insights from the Global C-suite Study – The CEO Perspective.* Retrieved from https://www-01.ibm.com/common/ssi/cgi-bin/ssialias?htmlfid=GBE03719USEN&

7   Amabile, T. M., Conti, R., Coon, H., Lazenby, J. and Herron, M. (1996). Assessing the work environment for creativity. *Academy of Management Journal* 39(5), 1154–84.

8   Craft, A. (2002). *Creativity and Early Years Education*. London: Continuum.

9   Sawyer, K. (2017, 7 August) Creative Collaboration at Apple Park Retrieved from https://keithsawyer.wordpress.com/2017/08/07/creative-collaboration-at-apple-park/

10 Kinson, S. (2008). 'Markus Zusak', *The Guardian*. 28 March. Retrieved from http://www.theguardian.com/books/2008/mar/28/whyiwrite

11 Chen, M. H. and Kaufmann, G. (2008). Employee creativity and R&D: a critical review. *Creativity and Innovation Management* 17(1), 71–6.

12 Burkus, D. (2014). *The Myths of Creativity: The Truth About How Innovative Companies and People Generate Great Ideas*. (First edition) San Francisco: Jassey-Bass, P. John Wiley & Sons, 2013.

13 Csikszentmihalyi, M. (1996). *Creativity: Flow and the Psychology of Discovery and Invention*. New York: Harper Collins Publishers, p. 23.

14 Greene, M. (2001). *Variations on a Blue Guitar: The Lincoln Center Institute Lectures on Aesthetic Education*. Teachers College Press, p. 6.

15 Lindström, M. (2017). *Small Data: the Tiny Clues that Uncover HugeTrends*. London: John Murray Learning, p, 14.

16 Greene, M. (2001). *Variations on a Blue Guitar*, p. 6.

17 Abramović, M. (2012). *The Abramović Method*. Rome: Ore Cultura, p. 24.

18 Narev, I. (2015). In M. Drummond, Why Commonwealth Bank Chief Ian Narev wants you to stare at blank walls. *AFR weekend*, Retrieved 26 February 2016 from http://www.afr.com/lifestyle/arts-and-entertainment/why-commonwealth-band-chief-ian-narev-wants-you-to-stare-at-blank-walls-20150626-ghyadr

19 Ibid.

20 Dobbs, M. E. (2016). Tesla, SpaceX, and the Quest for a fantastic future. *Journal of Applied Management and Entrepreneurship* 21(1), 83.

21 Freshwater, H. (2001). The ethics of indeterminacy: Theatre de Complicite's 'mnemonic'. *New Theatre Quarterly*, 17, 212–18.

22 Alexander, Catherine, Natasha Freedman and Victoria Gould (2007). *A Disappearing Number resource pack*. Retrieved from www.complicite.org

23 Trueman, M. (2013). Interview: the founders of Complicité. *Financial Times*, 25May. Retrieved from http://www.ft.com/cms/s/2/6afbab60-c14c-11e2-9767-00144feab7de.html

24 Abbott, S. (2014). Simon Burney's ambitious pursuit of the pure maths play. *Interdisciplinary Science Reviews* 39(3), 224–37.

25 Greene, M. (2011). 'Imagination, Inquiry and Innovation'. Conference at College of New Rochell, p. 62.

26 The Creative Organizations Index has been developed by 4C Organizational Transformation and details are available on the website 4corganizations.org

27 Isaksen, S. G., Lauer, K. J. and Ekvall, G. (1999). Situational outlook questionnaire: a measure of the climate for creativity and change. *Psychological Reports* 85(2), 665–74.

Chapter 6

1 Jung, J. C. (2017). Case Study: Volkswagen's Diesel Emissions Scandal. *Thunderbird International Business Review* 59(1), 127–37.

2 Ibid.

3 Jung, J. C. (2017) Case Study, p.

4 Fook, J., Collington, V., Ross, F., Ruch, G. and West, L. (eds) (2015). *Researching Critical Reflection: Multidisciplinary Perspectives*. Routledge, p. 48.

5 We have changed names and details to protect the identity of this organization.

6 One of the problems with terms such as 'critical' (in the same way as creativity) is that it lacks definitional clarity (it is an aerosol word) effecting its meanings and applications. Henry Mintzberg ('What do we mean by "Critical"?', an oral presentation at the Academy of Management meeting in Hawaii, 2005) identifies nine distinct uses of the term critical:

   1 Questioning
   2 Key (as in unlocking)
   3 Fault finding
   4 Judicial
   5 Providing textual variance
   6 Pertaining to crisis
   7 Crucial
   8 Grave uncertainty (like a critical injury)
   9 From physics, the moment at which a substance changes form.

   We see several relevant meanings of critical but particularly 'questioning' and 'key (as in unlocking)'.

7 Habermas, J. (1978). *Knowledge and Human Interests* (2nd edn). London: Heinemann, p. 42.

8 Fook, J., White, S., Gardner, F. (2006). 'Critical reflection: a review of contemporary literature and understandings'. In S. White, J. Fook and F. Gardener (eds), *Critical Reflection in Health and Social Care*. Maidenhead: Open University Press, pp. 3–20.

9 Ibid., p. 29.

10 Ibid., p. 9.

11 Ibid.

12 Scriven, M. and Paul, R. (1987). 'Critical Thinking as Defined by the National Council for Excellence in Critical Thinking'. In, 8th Annual International Conference on Critical Thinking and Education Reform, Rohnert Park, CA.

13 Fook, White and Gardner (2006). 'Critical reflection', p. 7.

14 Fook and co-workers (2015). *Researching Critical Reflection*, p. 99.

15 Fook, J. (2012). *Social Work: A Critical Approach to Practice*. London: SAGE, p. 232.

16 *Cambridge Dictionary* (2018). Unlearn. Retrieved from https://dictionary.cambridge. org/dictionary/english/unlearn

17 Mezirow, J. (1990). How critical reflection triggers transformative learning. Fostering critical reflection. *Adulthood* , 1–20.

18 Ghaye, T. (2010). In what ways can reflective practices enhance human flourishing? *Reflective Practice* 11(1), 1–7.

19 Fook, J., Psoinos, M. and Sartori, D. (2015). Evaluation studies of critical reflection. In Fook, J., Collington, V., Ross, F., Ruch, G. and West, L. (eds), *Researching Critical Reflection: Multidisciplinary Perspectives*. New York: Routledge, pp. 90–104.

Chapter 7

1   Buell, R. W. and Otazo, A. (2016). 'IDEO: Human-centred Service Design, Case Study'. Harvard Business School, 29 January, p. 6.

2   Ibid.

3   Ibid., p. 2.

4   Ibid.

5   Eisenberg, E. M. (2009). 'Organizational Communication Theories'. In S. Littlejohn and K. Foss (eds), *Encyclopedia of Communication Theory*, London: Sage, pp. 700–5.

6   Powell, A. (2016). 'How IDEO Designers Persuade Companies to Accept Change'. *Harvard Business Review*, 17 May, Retrieved from: https://hbr.org/2016/05/how-ideo-designers-persuade-companies-to-accept-change

7   Buell, R. W. and Otazo, A. (2016). IDEO: Human-centred Service Design, p. 7.

8   Ibid.

9   Ibid., p. 8.

10 Ibid., p. 9.

11 McLuhan, M. (1964/1994). *Understanding Media: The Extensions of Man*. Cambridge, MA: First MIT Press Edition. p. 7.

12 Campos, M. N. (2009). 'Critical Constructivism'. In S. Littlejohn, and K. Foss (eds), *Encyclopedia of Communication Theory*, London: Sage, p. 218.

13 Bernanke, B. (2015). 'More Talk, More Action'. *The Economist*, 17 October, p. 37.

14 Warren, J. (2009). 'Critical Communication Pedagogy'. In S. Littlejohn, and K. Foss (eds), *Encyclopedia of Communication Theory*, London: Sage, p. 215.

15 Rushdie, S. (2017). Shades of Red and Blue. *The Guardian* supported event, ethics centre event held at New York Public Library, 1 April.

16 Freire, P. (1970/2006). *Pedagogy of the Oppressed (30th Anniversary Ed.).* New York: Continuum, p. 90.

17 Orwell, G. (1949). *1984*. New York: Signet Classics, p. 81.

18 Buell, R. W. and Otazo, A. (2016). IDEO, p. 3.

19 IDEO (2015). *Little Book of IDEO*. Retrieved from https://www.ideo.com/post/the-little-book-of-ideo

20 Ibid., p. 13.

21 Ruck, K., Welch, M. and Menara, B. (2017). Employee voice: An antecedent to organisational engagement? *Public Relations Review* 43(5), 904–14.

22 Giddens, A. (1991). *Modernity and Self-identity: Self and Society in the Late Modern Age*. Stanford: Stanford University Press.

23 Ibid., p. 10.

24 OpenIDEO (2011). '7 Tips On Better Brainstorming', *OpenIDEO*, 23 February. Retrieved from https://challenges.openideo.com/blog/seven-tips-on-better-brainstorming

25 Bilton, C. (2007). *Management and Creativity: From Creative Industries to Creative Management*. Malden, MA: Blackwell Publishing, p. 63.

26 Hecht, M. (2009). 'Communication Theory of Identity'. In S. Littlejohn, and K. Foss (eds), *Encyclopedia of Communication Theory*, Los Angeles: Sage, pp. 139–41.

27 Conquergood, D. (2013). 'Beyond the text: Toward a performative cultural politics'. In E. P. Johnson (ed), *Cultural Struggles: Performance, Ethnography, Praxis*, Ann Arbor, MI: University of Michigan Press, pp. 33–47.

28 Lévi-Strauss, Claude (1962). *La Pensée sauvage*. Paris. English translation as *The Savage Mind* (Chicago, 1966).

29 Ibid., p. 11.

30 Holmes, D. (2005). *Communication Theory: Media, Technology and Society*. London: SAGE.

31 IDEO (2018). IDEO. Retrieved from: https://www.ideo.com

32 Ibid.

33 Ibid.

34 Sternberg, R. J. (2003). *Wisdom, Intelligence, and Creativity, Synthesized*. New York: Cambridge University Press.

35 Ibid., p. 109.

36 Conger, J. A. (2013). 'The Necessary Art of Persuasion'. In *HBR's 10 Must Reads On Communication*, Boston, MA: Harvard Business Review Press.

37 Hecht, M. L., Warren, J., Jung, J. and Krieger, J. (2004). 'Communication theory of identity'. In W. B. Gudykunst (ed.), *Theorizing About Intercultural Communication*. Newbury Park, CA: Sage, pp. 257–78.

38 Humphrey, J. (2018). *Impromptu: Leading in the Moment*. New Jersey: John Wiley and Sons.

39 Salazar, A. J., (2002). Self-organizing and complexity perspectives of group creativity. *New Directions in Group Communication*, 179–99.

40 Salazar, A. J. (2009). 'Creativity in Groups'. In S. Littlejohn and K. Foss (eds), *Encyclopedia of Communication Theory*, London: Sage, p. 212.

41 Ibid.

42 Fassett, D. and Warren, J. (2007). *Critical Communication Pedagogy*. London: Sage.

43 Hecht, M. L., Warren, J., Jung, J. and Krieger, J. (2004), 'Communication theory of identities'; Yingling, J. (2004). *A Lifetime of Communication: Transformations Through Relational Dialogues*, Mahwah, NJ: Lawrence Erlbaum.

44 Buell, R. W. and Otazo, A. (2016). IDEO: Human-centred Service Design, p. 7.

45 Freire, P. (1970/2006). *Pedagogy of the Oppressed*.

46 Warren, J. (2009). 'Critical Communication Pedagogy'.

47 Campos (2009). 'Critical Constructivism'.

48 Morreale, S. P. and Pearson, J. C. (2008). Why communication education is important: the centrality of the discipline in the 21st century. *Communication Education* 57(2): 224–40.

Chapter 8

1 Berkowitz, S. A., Brown, P., Brotman, D. J., Deutschendorf, A., Dunbar, L., Everett, A., Hickman, D., Howell, E., Purnell, L., Sylvester, C. and Zollinger, R. (2016). Case study: Johns Hopkins Community Health Partnership: a model for transformation. *Healthcare* 4(4): 264–70.

2 Ibid.

3 Ibid., p. 270.

4 John-Steiner, V. (2000). *Creative Collaboration*. New York: Oxford University Press.

5   Ibid., p. 188.

6   Paulus, P. (2000). Groups, teams, and creativity: the creative potential of idea generating groups. *Applied Psychology* 49(2), 237–62.

7   re:Work (2015). *Identify Dynamics of Effective Teams*. Retrieved from https://rework. withgoogle.com/guides/understanding-team-effectiveness/steps/identify-dynamics-of-effective-teams/

8   Ibid.

9   Gardner, H. K. (2016). *Smart Collaboration: How Professionals and their Firms Succeed in Breaking Down Silos*. Harvard: Harvard Business Review Press.

10   Berkowitz and co-workers (2016). Case study: J-CHiP, p. 265.

11   Ibid., p. 264.

12   Pisano, G. P. and Verganti, R. (2008). Which kind of collaboration is right for you. *Harvard Business Review* 86(12), 78–86.

13   Liu, J. and Brody, P. (2016). Is Collaboration the New Innovation? *Harvard Business Review*, 11 November, p. 7. Retrieved from https://hbr.org/2016/11/is-collaboration-the-new-innovation

14   Paulus, P. B. and Nijstad, B. A. (2003). *Group Creativity: Innovation through Collaboration*. New York: Oxford University Press.

15   Ibid.

16   Moran, S. and John-Steiner, V. (2004). 'How collaboration in creative work impacts identity and motivation'. In D. Miell and K. Littleton (eds), *Collaborative Creativity: Contemporary Perspectives*. London: Free Association Books, pp. 11–25.

17   Ibid., p. 11.

18   Daniels, J. (2015). Perspectives from a General Counsel. *Harvard Law School* 1(6), Retrieved from https://thepractice.law.harvard.edu/article/perspectives-from-a-general-counsel/

19   Gardner, H. K. (2015). 'Why it Pays to Collaborate'. *American Lawyer*, 9 March, p. 3.

20   Tett, G. (2015). *The Silo Effect: The Peril of Expertise and the Promise of Breaking Down Barriers*. New York: Simon and Schuster.

21   Ibid., p. x.

22   Sawyer, K. (2007). *Group Genius: The Creative Power of Collaboration*. New York: Basic Books, p. 7.

23   Hoever, I. J., Van Knippenberg, D., Van Ginkel, W. P. and Barkema, H. G. (2012). Fostering team creativity: perspective taking as key to unlocking diversity's potential. *Journal of Applied Psychology* 97(5), 982.

24 Moran, S. and John-Steiner, V. (2004). 'How collaboration in creative work impacts identity and motivation', p. 19.

25 Brown, B. (2012). *Daring Greatly: How the Courage to Be Vulnerable Transforms the Way We Live, Love, Parent, and Lead.* New York: Avery.

26 American poet Edwin Markham (1852–1940).

27 Pierse, L. (1995). *Theatresports Down Under: A Guide for Coaches and Players.* Kensington, N.S.W.: Improcorp Australia, p. 39.

28 Moran, S. and John-Steiner, V. (2004). 'How collaboration in creative work impacts identity and motivation', p. 21.

29 Webb, N. M. (2013). 'Information processing approaches to collaborative learning'. In C. Hmelo-Silver, C. Chinn, C. Chan and A. O'Donnell (eds), *The International Handbook of Collaborative Learning.* New York: Routledge, pp. 19–40.

30 Morgan, J. (2018). Analytic services how collaboration wins: leadership, benefits, and best practices. *Harvard Business Review*, p. 3. Retrieved from https://hbr.org/resources/pdfs/comm/citrix/HowCollaborationWins.pdf

31 Storey, H. and Joubert, M. (2004). The emotional dance of creative collaboration. In D. Miell and K. Littleton (eds), *Collaborative Creativity, Contemporary Perspectives*, London: Free Association Books, p. 47.

32 John-Steiner, V. (2000). *Creative Collaboration.*

33 Webb, N. M. (2013). 'Information processing approaches to collaborative learning'.

34 Janis, I. (1972). *Victims of Group Think: A Psychological Study of Foreign-policy Decisions and Fiascos.* Boston: Houghton Mifflin, p. 9.

35 Nemeth, C. J. and Nemeth-Brown, B. (2003). *Better than Individuals? The Potential Benefits of Dissent and Diversity for Group Creativity: Innovation through Collaboration.* Oxford: Oxford University Press.

36 Isaksen, S. G., Lauer, K. J. and Ekvall, G. (1999). Situational Outlook Questionnaire: A measure of the climate for creativity and change. *Psychological Reports* 85(2), 665–74.

37 John-Steiner, V. (2000). *Creative Collaboration.*

38 Scaffolding is an education term to describe the support provided to 'construct' learning. A scaffold provides processes, metalanguage and tasks to engage, facilitate, guide and deepen learning. Scaffolds for learning should encourage deep understanding of essential principals and fundamental structures in knowledge and processes. Like a building scaffold, the scaffolds are extended and dismantled as the learning is understood, practised and developed. Our organisation develops 'scaffolding' as strategies and processes to learn the 4C approaches described in this book.

39 Glaveanu, V. P. (2011). How are we creative together?: comparing sociocognitive and sociocultural answers. *Theory & Psychology* 21(4), 473–92.

40 Ibid. Retrieved from http://eprints.lse.ac.uk/38611/1/How%20are%20we%20 %creative%20together%20(isero).pdf, p. 13.

41 Moran, S. and John-Steiner, V. (2004). 'How collaboration in creative work impacts identity and motivation', p. 12.

42 Ibid., p. 18.

43 re:Work. (2015). *Identify Dynamics of Effective Teams.*

44 Storey, H. and Joubert, M. (2004). The emotional dance of creative collaboration, p. 49.

45 Ibid., pp. 47–8.

46 John-Steiner, V. (2000). *Creative Collaboration*, pp. 81 and 187.

47 Berkowitz and co-workers. (2016). Case study, p. 270.

48 John-Steiner, V. (2000). *Creative Collaboration*, p. 204.

Chapter 9

1 Bersin, J., McDowell, T., Rahnema, A. and Durme, V. D. (2017). 'The Organisation of the Future: Arriving Now'. *Deloitte Insights*, 28 February. Retrieved from https://www2. deloitte.com/insights/us/en/focus/human-capital-trends/2017/organization-of-the-future.html

2 Ibid., p. 2.

3 Sardar, Z. (2010). Welcome to postnormal times. *Futures*, 42(5), 435.

4 Guy, J. M., ed. (2007). *The Complete Works of Oscar Wilde: Volume IV: Criticism: Historical Criticism, Intentions, The Soul of Man.* Oxford: Oxford University Press, p. 25.

5 Mezirow, J. (1981). A critical theory of adult learning and education. *Adult Education* 32(1), 3–24.

6 Fullan, M. (2014). *Leading in a Culture of Change: Personal Action Guide and Workbook.* California: Jossey-Bass, p. 1.

7 Ibid., p. 109.

8 Muller, J. Z. (2018). *The Tyranny of Metrics.* Princeton: Princeton University Press.

9 Ibid., p. 17.

10 Muller, J. Z. (2018). The tyranny of metrics. *The Chronicle of Higher Education*, 21 January. Retrieved from https://www.chronicle.com/article/The-Tyranny-of-Metrics/242269

INDEX

Figures and tables are indicated by *f* and *t* respectively